Presenting with Style

Advanced Strategies for Superior Presentations

Ellen Dowling, PhD
Michael Dowling, PhD

Writers Club Press

San Jose New York Lincoln Shanghai

Presenting with Style
Advanced Strategies for Superior Presentations

Published by Writers Club Press
an imprint of iUniverse.com, Inc.

For information address:
iUniverse.com, Inc.
620 North 48th Street
Suite 201
Lincoln, NE 68504-3467
www.iuniverse.com

ISBN: 0-595-09486-4

Printed in the United States of America

To our families and friends, and especially—to our students.

*It will be all right when what you have to say
is more important than the fact that your knees
are knocking.*
Eleanor Roosevelt

*The best thing about a career in comedy is that
if you fail, nobody's going to laugh at you.*
Anonymous

Dying is easy; comedy is hard.
David Garrick, 18th century actor

*Death, on the other hand, is one of the few things
that can be done easier lying down.*
Woody Allen

Give me immortality or give me death!
The Firesign Theater

Contents

Preface

A Fable for Our Time

This is the story of two business professionals who hated making presentations.

She hated them because she never felt like she had enough time to prepare, she always felt rushed, and she was never really sure that her presentations had any actual effect on her audiences. They always seemed to leave the room with the same opinions and conclusions they had when they came in. She felt that making a presentation was just a big waste of her time. Nobody seemed to care, so why should she?

He hated them because he found them boring—so boring that even he had trouble staying awake during his own presentation. But there was so much data to discuss, so much technical information to get across, how could his presentations NOT be boring? It would be so much easier if he could just send everyone a memo; why did he have to stand up and make these stupid presentations anyway?

This is also the story of their audiences—those poor drudges who are required to attend their presentations during staff meetings. Meetings, meetings, meetings. Mostly dumb. Security: (1 hr.) "Don't email secrets to the Russians." Sexual Harassment: (2 hrs.) "Don't tell dirty jokes." Pay: (3 hrs.) "We have a new pay system which you won't understand any better than the old one." And so on. Sometimes a drudge brings a book; other times they walk in, fill out their attendance card, and walk out. Too many boring presenters presenting information nobody really cares about.

(Ellen once asked an engineer at a large defense avionics company: "Did you sign a contract when you were hired in which you PROMISED always to be boring?" He laughed. Half-heartedly.)

So our story begins in the Land of Presentation Vicious Circles, populated by presenters who don't want to present, presenting to audiences who don't want to be there. And it's even worse if we tweak the scenarios a bit. Instead of presenters at a regular in-house staff meeting, how about a sales representative who dreads presenting to an audience of buyers who don't want to buy anything? Or a researcher who is not looking forward to sharing reams of data with conference attendees who'd rather be out sunning by the pool? Or a company CEO who can't wait to tell the stockholders that the price of the company's stock has taken a nosedive? Or an under-paid government official who anticipates being run out of town on a rail when the audience at a "public hearing" realizes that the government wants to do all the talking? Or a keynote speaker who has nothing interesting to say to group of sleepy diners after an unappetizing dinner?

Are these people doomed? If you see yourself here, are you doomed, too? Of course not! Repeat after us: "I don't HAVE to be boring. I don't HAVE to be boring. I don't HAVE to be boring."

Being Boring Does Not Add to Your Credibility

Ah, yes, but we think many professionals secretly think the opposite. We think many professionals are convinced that any deviation from the norm, however small, may undermine their professional credibility. We think this is why so many professional men still wear dark suits and ties and professional women wear dark suits and tie-like neck-things. Obviously the goal is to appear as clerical as possible. (And who ever associates priests and nuns with laughter?)

So in the Land of the Presentation Vicious Circles, you will see a clerically-garbed presenter, armed with a tall stack of overhead transparencies, march resolutely to the overhead projector, then turn military-style, place a data-filled, difficult to decipher, and out-of-focus transparency on the glass, adopt the front fig leaf position, and proceed to drone on monotonously for the next millennium (or what feels like a millennium to the audience). No slumping bodies, no glazed eyes, no twitching eyelids, no barely disguised yawns will stay Boring Presenter from his or her appointed tasks. (And it doesn't matter if Boring Presenters are using a state-of-the-art computer system with fabulous slides; they can still be just as sleep-inducing.)

And if you say to one of these Boring Presenters: "Gee, it looked like your audience was falling asleep in there," the reply will usually be: "They were? I didn't notice."

And then if you say to one of these Boring Presenters: "Maybe you could have added a little humor or drama or something to keep them interested in your subject," the reply will inevitably be: "Why should I? IT'S NOT MY JOB TO ENTERTAIN THEM."

No, but it IS your job to keep them awake. And a little style—a little humor, a little drama—will do exactly that. Without destroying your professional credibility.

Two major points to consider:

1. You can add style to a presentation without coming off like a clown.
2. No one ever attended a presentation HOPING to be bored.

Look at it this way: If you are the least little bit interesting, if you are the tiniest bit humorous, if you add the most minute splash of drama to your presentation, you're going to be a better presenter than 90% of the people you yourself are bored to death by every day. Adding style to a presentation is a very low-risk activity, and yet the return on investment is enormous.

Top Ten Reasons
Why You Should Add Style to Presentations

10. You'll find yourself actually looking forward to hearing yourself speak.
9. You'll establish rapport with your audience.
8. You'll make your audience like you (especially useful if you're trying to sell them something).
7. You'll help them remember even the driest of statistics.
6. You'll keep them awake.
5. You'll get glowing evaluations at the end of the session.
4. You'll make more money. (Not right away, of course, but eventually.)
3. You'll get promoted faster.
2. You'll defuse hostility.
1. You'll be asked to speak again!

We understand that many of you would not see Number 1 as a real benefit. After all, if you don't like making presentations now, why should you ever like making MORE of them? Ah, but if all the other benefits kick in for you (and we believe they will), then you WILL enjoy making presentations more, and, hence, you will want to make more of them. And, likewise, your audiences will want you back for more. Happy ever after, you will have arrived in the Land of the Opposite of the Presentation Vicious Circles, where the presenters are dynamic and the audiences actually stay awake, learn something, and come back for more.

But before you can get there from here, you have to be certain that you are even qualified to start on the journey. You must first pass the

Qualified Reader Self-Test

Are you qualified to read this book? Find out by answering yes or no to the questions below.

Question	Yes	No	
1. Have you presented before? At least several times?			
2. Do you wish that you had done a better job?			
3. Are you tired of being tied to the podium?			
4. Do you wish you had the guts to make a presentation *without* any audio-visual aids?			
5. Do you cringe when you see yourself present on videotape?			
6. Would you like to be a funnier presenter? Would you like to make your audience laugh once in a while?			
7. Do you wish you could just knock 'em dead?			
8. Do you wonder what it would be like to receive a standing ovation?			
9. Would you like to keep everyone in your audience awake for your entire presentation?			
10. Would you like them to remember all your most important points?			
11. Are you tired of being upstaged by your own transparencies or slides?			
12. Would you like to know if your personal presentation style is one that really works for you?			
13. Would you like to "pump up" your presentations with humorous and/or dramatic stories and anecdotes?			
14. Would you like to be in great demand as a presenter?			
15. Would you like to stop answering yes or no to questions?			

If you answered "yes" to all of the questions above, then you are exactly the sort of reader for whom we wrote this book.

[Note: If you answered "No" to any of the questions, then you're not ready to read this book. Don't even try. We have ways of finding you out.]

Ideal Reader Profile (Here's Who We Think You Are)

You're a professional, an expert in your field. Your job requires you to make presentations frequently. You've been doing so for a number of years. You've taken a basic "Effective Presentations" course. You've been videotaped. You've scanned a couple of books on the subject. You're really doing OK.

But the other day you attended a session somewhere where the presenter really knocked your socks off. And you said to yourself, "Why can't I do that?"

Well, we think you *can* do that. And we don't care if you think you're basically a drab, humorless sort of person (although we do feel sorry for your spouse). We believe there are techniques you can use to become a dynamic, interesting speaker, no matter how static and boring you may be in the "real life" of your living room.

We believe there's hope for you. And obviously you do, too, or else you wouldn't be reading this.

So What Can You Learn from This Book?

Ten Useful Things:

1. How to work with what you already have going for you.

We're not going to ask you to do anything that would make you look silly. We're not going to tell you to add magic tricks to your presentations or play games with your audience if you're not comfortable with that. Pyrotechnical hoo-hah can be spectacular, but only under the right conditions.

What we ARE going to do is ask you to determine which of five basic presentation styles most closely matches your own preferred style. Then we'll ask you to think about how you can modify your own style to perform best under varying circumstances (and add a little hoo-hah, if appropriate).

2. How to illustrate your presentations with style.

If you're going to be funny, you have to have something funny to say. If you're going to be dramatic, likewise. So where do you get this funny and/or dramatic stuff?

In this book, you'll learn how to create and develop your *own* humorous material, to accompany your *own* personal style. We'll steer you away from joke telling and toward the dynamic art of storytelling. And, because one size does NOT fit all, we'll show you how to *tailor* your material to fit a variety of audiences.

3. How to design and time a presentation with style.

Once you've assembled your stuff, we'll show you how to put it all together in a way that makes it easy for you to time your presentation accurately and adjust your presentation plan to take advantage of any "on the spot" opportunities to add style.

No notes, please. No index cards. And (perish the thought!) no memorizing. No boring "agendas" on blurry overheads. The *Presentation Diamond*™ will help you come across as a polished *extemporaneous* speaker. Planned spontaneity is the name of the game here, and it's a sure-fire knock-your-socks-off technique. Plus, you'll always end ON TIME.

4. How to prepare for the actual presentation…

…even when you have no time to prepare. Like when your boss waltzes into your cubicle, hands you a stack of overheads, and nonchalantly announces, "Hey—I can't make the briefing to OUR MAJOR CUSTOMER at 10 o'clock. Got a conflict. You do it." And it's 9:45 when she says this.

On the other side, we'll also show you how to rehearse for a presentation in an efficient, focused manner, so that you don't spend 6 weeks (if you've got that kind of time) obsessing and fretting unnecessarily.

And that's not all: In this book you'll also get some useful information about taking control of the space you're presenting in, as well as a couple of techniques for manipulating the dynamics of the space. A dynamic presentation is all about energy, and we can show you how to focus this energy to achieve your presentation's objective.

5. How to polish your presentation style.

No, no, no, don't look at us like that. We're not going to try to turn you into Laurence Olivier or Sarah Bernhardt. (Although it wouldn't hurt to borrow a little bit of their style.)

But we are going to urge you to develop your primary audio-visual aid—your own body—so that you become the most interesting thing in the room to look at.

So we're going to throw in a little "acting class for presenters" here: Do you speak loudly enough so that your audience, no matter how large, can hear you? If not, we have some techniques for you. Do you speak too fast, too slow, in a monotone, or with an accent? Ditto the techniques bit. Don't know what to do with your hands? Ditto. Afraid to come out from behind the podium? Yes, we have help for that, too.

And, as an extra added attraction bonus, we'll tell you exactly what you need to do to get a standing ovation.

6. How to "inter-act" with your audience.

Rehearse all you want in the privacy of your living room or office—eventually you're going to be faced with a real, live audience. And this real, live audience may be very different from your spouse, or children, or friends, or pets, or whomever you tried presenting to in rehearsal. For one thing, they may not already love you and want you to do well. If you're lucky, they may just not know you at all. If you're unlucky, they may already hate your guts.

We'll show you some specific techniques for establishing and maintaining rapport with your audience, so that you are both consciously aware that you're in the situation together.

7. How to "stay in character" when things go wrong.

This is the nightmare side of Chapter 6: Not only are you surprised by your audience, but you also feel threatened by them. (Perhaps it's the fact that they have all risen and are slowly walking toward you? That could be a hint.) Or—and this is even worse for some people—it's just that things around you are falling apart, the center is not holding, and you are beginning to feel like a falcon who cannot hear the falconer. (A little allusion for you literary types.)

These potential horror stories can be rewritten with happy endings. Some involve the strategic use of humor to defuse aggression, sidestep embarrassment, and get the presentation back on track. We'll show you how.

8. How to apply what you've learned to 7 different kinds of presentations.

Sales Presentations: How to use storytelling to clinch the sale.

Briefings: How to make them truly **brief**, and enjoyable as well as informative.

Conference Presentations: How to enliven even the dullest academic thesis.

Keynote Speeches: How to kick the conference into high gear.

After-Dinner Talks: How to be more interesting than the chocolate mousse.

Public Hearings: How to defuse aggression with tact and rapport.

Instructional Sessions: How to use humor and drama to help them remember what you teach them.

9. How to continuously improve your style.

No one ever finally becomes a "perfect" speaker. Indeed, just when you think, "A ha! I've got it now," along comes a new audience that refuses to laugh at your best funny stories, falls asleep during your most animated explanation, or just plain doesn't like your style. "What could I have done," you wonder, "to turn them around?"

We have ways of making you improve—three main techniques, in fact, and an additional seven **Quick Tips**. And we end it all by asking you to complete your own personal "Action Plan" for continuous success.

10. Research and Resources.

In this final chapter we'll highlight some supplementary sources for your own continuous improvement. Here you'll find a few of our favorite things to enhance your learning enjoyment—some other books to read, some stories to use, some web sites to visit.

Before we end this preface, there's one more thing we want to tell you about how to read this book. Periodically you will see a box that looks like this:

Quick Tip:
These boxes contain tips that you can use immediately to enliven your next presentation. Just flip through this book and pull these out whenever you need them.

The Rest of the Story

So let's revisit our Bored (and Boring) Presenters in the Land of the Presentation Vicious Circles and remind them that they'll never find their way out of the maze of monotonous speeches unless they remember the secret words: "We don't HAVE to be boring."

It's all a matter of attitude and technique. You supply the attitude, and we'll supply the technique.

Off we go—

Start from Where You are

This above all: to thine own self be true,
And it must follow, as the night the day,
Thou canst not then be false to any man.
Polonius, in Hamlet

Polonius is a comic character, an old fuddy-duddy prone to meddling and manipulating, but his advice to his son Laertes is sound and serious. It is important to be true to yourself, to feel centered in your own sense of who you are and what you want to achieve. If you are naturally an animated, super-energetic storyteller, it's not going to be difficult for you to *act* like an animated, super-energetic storyteller during a presentation. If, on the other hand, you are an unanimated, subdued data-relater, then it is indeed going to be difficult for you to act like an animated, super-energetic storyteller during a presentation. In fact, if you try to act the opposite of your natural personality, you will most likely come across as false and pretentious. To be true to yourself as a presenter, you've got to build on the style you already possess.

Think about this for a minute: Are you the same person in front of the audience for a business presentation in the afternoon that you are in front of your tv set later that evening? Well, yes, you say (hesitantly). Ah, but do you display the same *style*? Do you move the same, talk the same, look the same? Well, sort of, you say. I'm flopped out on the couch instead of standing in front of an audience, I'm mumbling to my

1

spouse, "Honey, where's the remote?" instead of discussing future investment trends, and I'm dressed in my jammies instead of my business suit, but *basically* I'm the same person.

Well, sure, that's what we've been telling you: You can be—nay, should be—basically the same person inside. But on the outside, what others see is your *style*—your public self. And that style is yours to manipulate to meet the needs of changing situations. "All the world's a stage," Shakespeare reminds us. And we all play many parts throughout our daily lives.

If you're feeling a bit skeptical, think of it this way: Has a loved one ever asked you how you liked their new haircut, and you thought it was horrible, but you said it was "interesting"? If you are a consultant, have you ever had to tell a client, "Thank you so much for deciding to go with one of my competitors" with a big smile on your face? No acting there? Let's face it—we're acting MOST of the time. (It's the main reason we still don't have video phones. No one really wants the other person to be able to see what they look like as they say, "Well, I'm sorry we couldn't come to an agreement, but I want to thank you anyway for your time.")

So when we talk about "building a personal style," we are referring to the process of enhancing the natural attributes you already possess and making them stage worthy—that is, suitable for public presentation. And we are talking about a *physical* process here, building a style from the outside in. We don't care how you feel inside. Your audience doesn't care, because they can't see inside you. They won't know you're feeling nervous if you don't LOOK nervous. They just see the end result, the physical style.

A little theater history interlude: The great teacher of modern acting, Constantin Stanislavsky (1863-1938), addressed this very process in his 1949 book, *Building a Character*. It doesn't matter, Stanislavsky said, how wonderfully developed your internal image of yourself is: "If you do not use your body, your voice, a manner of speaking, walking, moving, if you do not find a form of characterization which corresponds to the image, you probably cannot convey to others its inner, living spirit." And here's the good news: Stanislavsky said that this characterization can be achieved by means of "purely technical, mechanical, simple external tricks." No psychological delving necessary. (There's more on Stanislavsky, if you're interested, in Chapter 10.)

How simple? It goes like this: First, decide what kind of style you already possess. Then investigate how many ways you can adapt that style to fit the needs of a variety of audiences and speaking situations. The following *Presenter's Style Profile* will help you determine where you are now and where you want to go.

Presenter's Style Profile

Instructions: For each of the groups listed below, you have 10 points to distribute between five choices. Rate your preference for each choice by giving it a score from 0 to 10. A score of 0 means that you dislike that particular response, or feel more strongly about the other responses. A score of 10 means you strongly prefer that response or dislike the other responses. All five scores must add up to 10. (Do not use fractions.)

Example:
    If I have a choice of ice cream flavors, I prefer
      6 A. chocolate
      2 B. vanilla
      1 C. tutti-fruiti
      0 D. bubble gum
      1 E. licorice

1. When I am making a presentation, I prefer to
    A. Use stories and anecdotes to persuade my audience.
    B. Use many different kinds of audio-visual aids to explain my points.
    C. Use drama and humor to make my presentation come alive.

    D. Use a few simple aids, like a flip chart or a white board, to record key points.

    E. Use verbal dexterity to increase my audience's ability to remember what I said.

2. When I am making a presentation, I prefer to
    A. Use my hands to illustrate key points.
    B. Use a pointer or a marker to indicate key points.
    C. Use my entire body to dramatize key points.
    D. Use a pen/marker to record others' key points.
    E. Use my words alone to illustrate key points.

3. When I am making a presentation I prefer to
    A. Speak from notes prepared around a specific theme.
    B. Speak from a logically organized outline.
    C. Memorize key bits.
    D. Establish an agenda with my audience.
    E. Read a prepared speech.

4. When I am making a presentation I prefer to
    A. Elicit belief and commitment from my audience.
    B. Elicit comments and questions from my audience.
    C. Elicit laughter and applause from my audience.
    D. Elicit decisions and recommendations from my audience.
    E. Elicit respect and agreement from my audience.

5. When I make a presentation, my goal is to
    A. Make my audience respond emotionally.
    B. Make my audience learn new information.
    C. Make my audience laugh.
    D. Make my audience articulate their own ideas.
    E. Make my audience believe in my credibility.

6. When I make a presentation, I prefer to
    A. Use my voice to capture my audiences' imaginations.
    B. Use my voice to convey information.
    C. Use my voice to amuse and amaze my audience.

D. Use my voice to setup and debrief the session.

E. Use my voice to persuade my audience of my sincerity.

7. When I make a presentation, I prefer to

    A. Take my audience to a place beyond my control.

    B. Establish and maintain control of my audience's learning process.

    C. Establish and maintain control of my audience's emotions.

    D. Let my audience control the session.

    E. Establish and maintain control of my audience's perceptions.

8. When I make a presentation,

    A. I do not pay much attention to time.

    B. I organize my remarks to fit a pre-selected time period.

    C. I pay great attention to time and timing.

    D. I am the timekeeper.

    E. I time my remarks in advance.

9. When I make a presentation, I prefer to

    A. Use very little humor in my presentation.

    B. Use humor only to illustrate key learnings.

    C. Use humor as an end in itself.

    D. Let the humor come from the audience.

    E. Avoid humor entirely.

10. When I make a presentation, I prefer to

    A. Use stories and anecdotes to edify my audience.

    B. Use stories and analogies to explain complex ideas.

    C. Use stories and jokes to wake my audience up.

    D. Rarely use stories at all.

    E. Use real-life stories to persuade.

Now for the math part. Use the scoring sheet below to figure out your overall scores for each category.

Scoring Sheet for Presenter's Style Profile

Presentation Style	I	II	III	IV	V	VI	VII	VIII	IX	X	Totals
A.											
B.											
C.											
D.											
E.											
Totals (Each column must add up to 10):											Total (Must add up to 100):

Then list your scores in order of highest to lowest preference:

1.

2.

3.

4.

5.

Now, check your preferences against the Presentation Styles Analysis that follows:

Presentation Styles Analysis

A. Preacher

Description:

Preachers are high-intensity, emotion-driven speakers. They rarely use any audio-visual aids, preferring instead to use their bodies, particularly their hands, to illustrate their main points. They may employ a sort of sing-song vocal delivery, designed to stir the hearts, rather than the minds, of their listeners. They usually do not read their presentations (or sermons); rather, they speak from notes organized around a particular theme. Their primary goal is to elicit belief and commitment from their audiences; they want their audiences to respond to them emotionally. (Amen!) In that respect, they are not very much concerned with time constraints: They may go on as long as it takes to get their audience to a fever-pitch, perhaps to a state beyond their control. They rarely use humor in their presentations, since their subject matter is so serious, but they will use stories and anecdotes (parables) to bring their listeners to a fuller understanding of their message.

Strengths:

A good Preacher can change an audience's beliefs and attitudes. A good Preacher can motivate an audience to a high level of drive and commitment. He/she can figuratively set them on fire with purpose and dedication. A good Preacher is always needed at the start of a campaign, or when the doldrums have set in, or when people need to be re-charged and re-energized. A successful sales presentation always includes a high level of Preacher style.

Drawbacks:

Audiences don't always want to be preached at. In many situations, the Preacher's high intensity style can come across as too much, either too aggressive or just too corny. The same fire that can turn some people on will turn others off. Audiences wanting to learn information may also criticize a Preacher for not giving them anything concrete to hold on to.

Examples of Famous "Preachers":

Jesus Christ
Joan of Arc
Bill Clinton
Og Mandino

B. The Professor

Professors speak to impart knowledge. Thus, they usually place great store on using a variety of audio-visual aids to help their audience (their students) learn more effectively. They also rely more often than others on holding a pointer or a marker in their hands, so that they can be ready to point to a concept on the overhead screen or draw a diagram on the whiteboard. In general they prefer to speak from a prepared outline, organized rationally around a particular subject or "lesson plan." Many Professors employ the "Socratic Method" of presenting, asking questions of their students in order to lead them to their own self-discovery. They also encourage their students to make comments and ask questions in return. They do not usually pay much attention to their own vocal delivery, as long as students can hear them and achieve the goal of learning something. Through these behaviors, Professors exert fairly strict control over their students' learning process, and organize their lectures to fit the predetermined length of the class. While Professors may use a bit of humor here and there to illustrate a key learning, they usually prefer to use stories and analogies to explain complex ideas.

Strengths:

A little learning is a most useful thing, and Professors are pros when it comes to imparting knowledge. If an audience has come to the session to learn how to use the latest computer software or identify the reasons for the fall of the Roman Empire, then they will need a Professor to lead them to learning.

Drawbacks:

Under some circumstances, audiences will not appreciate being "lectured to" by anyone, especially if the audience already thinks they know all the answers. If ancient religious or age-old political beliefs are involved, for example, it will be very difficult for any Professor to teach the listeners something "new." Indeed, any such attempt to impart knowledge will be vigorously resisted.

And one more thing: Beware the speaker who tries to give an after-dinner talk in high Professor mode. (We feel ourselves nodding off just thinking about it.)

Examples of Famous "Professors":
Professor Kingsfield (from *The Paper Chase*)
Henry Kissinger
Norbert Weiner
S.I. Hayakawa
Tom Peters
Elizabeth Kubler-Ross

C. The Entertainer

Entertainers love to be loved. Perhaps that is why they so relish applause: It's a concrete sign of approval. The worst thing that can happen to an Entertainer is for the audience to fall asleep during his/her presentation. Entertainers take that as a personal insult. Thus, Entertainers go to great lengths to use humor and drama to make their presentations come alive. They don't need audio visuals to accomplish this, either; they prefer to use their entire bodies to make their points. Although Entertainers may prepare notes for their presentations, they are most concerned with memorizing key "bits"—stories, jokes, anecdotes—which they can sprinkle around to illustrate a point or just keep the energy level high. Entertainers truly love to make their audiences laugh, because they believe that laughter not only energizes an audience, but that it also helps them stay awake and remember key points more successfully. They spend much time working on their vocal delivery, in order to use a variety of voices throughout their presentation. (Entertainers, above all other presenters, abhor monotony.) This vocal dexterity also allows them to manipulate their audience's emotions throughout the presentation, a skill which also depends most importantly on a keen sense of timing. Humor can be an end in itself to an Entertainer, for if people are not paying attention, what's the point of speaking at all?

Strengths:

You want to make a dry, technical presentation less boring? Get an Entertainer to make it! Entertainers can make any subject interesting, can keep students awake during a long session, can keep after-dinner audiences from snoring after the dessert, can look great on television. In the kickoff to a new campaign, an Entertainer may be just what you need to get people whoopin' and hollarin'. If the audience is stressed out over something, an Entertainer may be able to calm them down with humor.

Drawbacks:

Humor is frequently not appropriate to the situation. Entertainers may offend people by telling insensitive "-ist" jokes (racist, sexist, etc.). Like Preachers, Entertainers can come across so intensely that they actually wear audiences out. Some cultures do not appreciate Entertainers at all in a learning situation. And sometimes an Entertainer's presentation can seem like a salad: A perfectly OK meal when you're expecting something light, but not very filling when you were hoping for lasagna.

Examples of Famous "Entertainers":

Mark Twain (See Chapter 10.)

Oscar Wilde

Bette Midler

Lily Tomlin

D. The Facilitator

Facilitators don't really make presentations so much as they help audience members (participants) articulate their own points of view. Thus, Facilitators don't really need a stage; they just need a room with a few audio-visual tools (like a flip chart) to record what the audience has to say. Since the focus of the session is not on them, but on their audience, they are not very concerned with what their bodies or voices are doing—they are more concerned with using a pen or marker to record others' comments. Facilitators rarely prepare their remarks beforehand; they prefer to devise an agenda with the audience. Facilitators are true participatory leaders. Their main objective is to help their audiences reach consensus on decisions and make recommendations. They don't need verbal pyrotechnics to accomplish this goal; they merely use their voices to set up and debrief the session. Facilitators are the timekeepers of a session, but they do not really control the flow or the outcomes—that's the audience's job. Any humor or storytelling usually comes from audience members, rarely from the Facilitators themselves.

Strengths:

Facilitators are like the motors in a smoothly-running engine: You don't much notice that they are there, and yet without them you would never get where you're going. For any session where the audience members are feeling upset or angry, a Facilitator will be much more adept at calming them down and reaching some sort of workable solution than the other presentation styles.

Drawbacks:

If you've come to the session to learn a particular skill, you are not going to be happy with someone who wants to start "from where you are." If there is not much opportunity for audience participation during the session, due to the technical skills nature of the subject, a Facilitator's laid-back, "so what do you want to do" style will not work at all. Indeed, participants unable to participate will probably disconnect entirely from the proceedings or nod off.

Examples of Famous "Facilitators":

There aren't any. The whole point of being a Facilitator is that the *group* is more important than the presenter.

E. The Orator

Orators LOVE to give speeches. They love to hear themselves speak. Words are powerful tools for Orators, and they use them deliberately. They believe that if they can just turn a phrase in a powerful way, they will have won their audience's undying interest and support. (It is thus no surprise that politicians are primarily Orators.) Since words are so important, Orators prefer to deliver a fully prepared speech, one that has been written (either by themselves or a speech writer) and rewritten, edited and re-edited, and rehearsed, rehearsed, rehearsed. The Orator's main goal is typically to gain the respect and attention of their audience in order to increase their credibility quotient. Orators tend to be great salespeople, and what they sell is sincerity. Control is very important to Orators, who, if they have to have some audience participation, prefer that their listeners hold their questions and comments until the end, at the formal question and answer period. Indeed, the Q&A session is the most nerve-wracking part of the presentation for Orators, because they can never be quite sure how long the audience will take to complete their part. Timing is critical to Orators. Rarely do Orators use humor in their presentations—too chancy. Rather, they prefer real-life stories that can grab their listeners' hearts.

Strengths:

Oratory is an ancient and noble art. In classical Greek and Roman times, Orators were praised for their ability to light up the sky with their rhetoric and poetry. When it is important to show the world that your company (or country) is the best in the biz, bar none, there is none better than an Orator to give the State of the Union speech.

Drawbacks:

If you're really interested in getting the facts and learning new information, you're going to be sorely disappointed by an Orator. Indeed, you'll probably complain that all you got was rhetoric—empty words and phrases, signifying nothing. And if you're looking for a participatory encounter with the speaker, forget it—you have to wait till the Q&A period, remember?

Examples of Famous "Orators":

Demosthenes

Dr. Martin Luther King, Jr.

John F. Kennedy

Barbara Jordan

If you're like most people, you're probably going to find that your preferred style is actually a mixture of the styles described above. If you're a trainer, for example, you may find yourself preaching a little to pump up your tired trainees, then later entertaining them a bit to keep them interested in a dry subject. Perhaps you'll facilitate some of the training session, then switch over to professor style to explain a new, complex process. Nothing like a little orator, either, to help them remember key words and phrases. Indeed, the very definition of a good trainer might be a presenter who exhibits all 5 styles at various points throughout the training session.

The most important aspects of your scores for you to think about are the extremes: Are you a high Professor, and a very low Facilitator? Perhaps you should try to relinquish the podium once in a while and encourage more participation among your participants. Are you a high Entertainer and a low Professor? This is not a bad thing to be if you are primarily an after-dinner speaker; if you're trying to become a trainer, you're going to need to provide real information, not just tell jokes. And even a Preacher might try to keep audiences awake and enthused by adding a little entertainment.

> ### Quick Tip:
> If you want to be truly daring, try adding a bit of your lowest-preferred style to your next presentation, and cutting back a bit on your highest-preferred style.

Self-Analysis Exercise: Building a Style

Traits of Your Highest-Ranked Style	Traits of Your Lowest-Ranked Style	Modifications You Wish to Make to Your Style

As you've probably suspected, different presentation styles are more or less effective depending on the kind of presentation you are making. We're going to discuss techniques for making different kinds of presentations in Chapter 8, but by way of a preview of coming attractions, we challenge you here to test your own awareness by filling out the chart below. Place an X beneath the style most effective for each type of presentation. If one style isn't enough, list the letters of a combination of styles in the last column on the right. (You might even want to assign %s.)

Type of Presentation	A: Preacher	B. Professor	C. Entertainer	D. Facilitator	E. Orator	Combination
Sales Presentation						
Briefing						
Conference Presentation						
Keynote Speech						
"After-Dinner Talk"						
Public Hearing						
Instructional Session						

Illustrate with style

No matter what style of presenter you are, or what kind of presentation you are making, you want your audience to remember what you say. Otherwise, what's the point? Why not just send them a memo instead?

So let's begin this section by determining what makes a presentation memorable. We'll start with you: Think back to one of the last presentations you attended, and list below the aspects that made it memorable.

[Note: If you remember attending a presentation, but you cannot remember what the speaker said, then we rest our case. If you can at least remember the speaker's name, be a pal and send him or her a copy of this book.]

Aspects that made the last presentation I saw memorable:

-
-
-
-
-
-
-
-

Now check your responses against those we have listed here:

- The presenter told funny jokes/stories. (Entertainer)
- The presenter told dramatic (not necessarily humorous) stories. (Entertainer)
- The presenter involved the audience in the presentation. (Professor, Facilitator)
- The presenter used his/her body to dramatize key points. (Preacher, Entertainer)
- The presenter used his/her voice to dramatize key points. (Preacher, Entertainer, Orator)
- The presenter used eye-catching audio-visual aids to illustrate key points. (Professor)
- The presenter used a dynamic rhetorical pattern. (Professor)
- The presenter invoked an emotional response from the audience. (Preacher, Orator, Entertainer)

There are other memorable behaviors, of course (you may have listed them yourself), but basically all memorable presenters fall into one (or more) of the following categories:

1. They present memorable material;
2. They present memorable material memorably;
3. They involve the audience in the presentation.

In this chapter we will focus on number 1: How to find or create memorable material for your presentations. In Chapter 5 we will discuss what are usually called "delivery techniques" for presenting your material in a memorable way. In Chapter 6 we will cover the art of interacting with your audience.

What makes the *content* of a presentation memorable? Very simple: something that creates pictures in your listeners' minds, something that forces them to visualize what you are saying. When your audience *sees* what you're talking about, they have a much better chance of remembering what you said.

"A picture is worth a thousand words," Anonymous once said. More recently, Don Keogh, former president of Coca-Cola, said, "A picture may be worth a thousand words, but a picture of a thousand words isn't worth much."

Now, many presenters—especially "technical" presenters—presume that since their topic is inherently boring, they have no alternative but to make a boring presentation. "My audience just wants the data," they say to themselves, "so that's all they're going to get—overhead after overhead, covered with data: lists, columns, graphs, charts, tables, etc., etc., etc. I believe that the facts should speak for themselves."

Who started this pernicious rumor? Who put out the word that technical professionals WANT to be bored at a presentation? We feel obligated here to say this again: If all you want to do is give your audience a mass of numbers, then WHY NOT JUST PUT THEM IN A WRITTEN REPORT? Why do you have to be there in person, if you're so sure than the facts will speak for themselves?

If a live human body is making a *presentation*, then we believe that body should have a purpose higher than that of just transmitting data—any machine can do that. You have been asked to *present* (not write) because, for some reason, your audience wants to receive the information filtered through your personal style. They paid (maybe) to see YOU, not just your slides. Your job is to go beyond their expectations, to give them an experience, not just a data dump.

This is not to say, of course, that audio visuals should not be used. On the contrary—they can be extremely useful tools for helping your audience remember your key points. We're just saying that they should not be the ENTIRE presentation.

There are two ways to avoid tedium and add style to the content of your presentation:

1. Create verbal illustrations.
2. Create visual illustrations.

A good presentation will usually include both.

Creating Verbal Illustrations

The word "illustrate" comes from the Latin *lustrare*, "to make bright." Similarly, the word "illuminate" (*luminare*) means "to light up." Truly, when you use illustrations to illuminate your key points, you can almost see those light bulbs clicking on in your listeners' minds.

There are a variety of verbal illustrations to choose from:

- jokes
- stories (especially real-life stories)
- examples and analogies (including parables)

Jokes

"A funny thing happened on the way to this presentation..."

Jokes are risky in most business presentations. They are often inappropriate. Or irrelevant. Or (worst-case scenario) offensive. On the other hand, jokes are also wonderful for relieving stress, for grabbing an audience's attention, for making a key point memorable. Still, there's that risk factor, depending on the kind of presentation you're making. After-dinner talk? Low-risk situation for jokes; in fact, your audience will probably expect some from you. Mid-morning briefing to upper management? Tremendously high-risk situation; your audience will most likely be taken aback by anything vaguely joke-like.

We know a minister who begins each of his Sunday services with a series of jokes (which he reads aloud from various joke books). Most of these jokes are true groaners, some are actually funny (and make us want to repeat them to others), all of them are (somewhat loosely) tied in to the theme of that day's sermon. This minister is obviously a Preacher with a high Entertainer quotient. He does not use jokes in the body of his talk, only at the beginning, at the podium, as a way of "warming up" his audience. His message is invariably one of joy and happiness—thus, laughter (even groaning) is an invaluable tool for helping his audience remember his sermon.

Jokes "work" for this minister. Would they work for Billy Graham? Would Martin Luther King, Jr.'s memorable "I have a dream" speech have "worked" better if he had started off with a few one-liners? Of course not. This is what we mean when we say that jokes are risky and not at all appropriate in certain situations or for certain presentation styles.

Plus, jokes are not all that easy to *make* work—the presenter must have the ability to tell jokes well, good timing and all. And since the pattern of a joke is so familiar to an audience—they can almost always see it coming—it's relatively easy to destroy the punch of a punch line by delivering it badly.

Quick Tip:
In general, you should avoid jokes unless you are 100% certain that the following three criteria are present:
1. The joke is tried and true funny. (You've told it several times before, and it always gets a laugh.)
2. The joke is actually relevant to a key point in your presentation.
3. The joke is completely, 100% not offensive to any person on any basis whatsoever.

Criteria number three is a real kicker, because it pretty much dooms any joke to white-bread blandness. But what's the alternative? Why risk alienating your audience? Yes, you want them to remember your presentation, but do you really want them to remember how much they despise you?

Let's test the criteria on a couple of jokes. You decide under what conditions the following five jokes would be suitable:

1. Two cannibals are having dinner. One of them turns to the other and says, "I hate my mother-in-law." The other cannibal says, "Well, just eat the noodles."

2. A Texan is sightseeing in London and he gets lost. He goes up to a very proper-looking British gentleman and asks, "Excuse me, sir, but could you tell me where the Tower of London is at?" The British gentleman looks down his nose at the Texan and replies, "My dear sir, here in the United Kingdom we take great care never to end our sentences with a preposition such as 'at'!" The Texan thinks about this for a minute, then says, "Well, OK then, can you tell me where the Tower of London is at, you jerk?"

3. A mathematician and a biologist were sharing a cell the night before their execution (for crimes unimaginable). The executioner came to ask for their last wishes. The mathematician glanced at the biologist and said, "I've been doing some work in mathematical biology, and I've got some interesting results. Before I die, would you arrange for me to give a seminar on my work?" "Sure," said the executioner, and he turned to the biologist. "Now, what would you like?" The biologist said, "I'd like to be executed before the seminar."

4. How many actors does it take to change a light bulb?

Nine. One to climb the ladder and replace the bulb, and eight to stand around grumbling, "That should be ME up there."

5. A bit of advice: Never throw cigar butts in urinals. They get soggy and are hard to light.

One last point about jokes: If your presentation style favors the Orator or Entertainer, you are probably already more comfortable about telling jokes than, say, a Facilitator. Some Professors are great joke-tellers; most should not even try. Indeed, the most memorable Professors we had in school were great story-, not joke-tellers. If you do not usually tell jokes in a relaxed, informal, friendly situation, surrounded by your loved ones, then what in the world would possess you to try to do so in a nerve-wracking, formal, potentially unfriendly situation, confronted by perfect strangers? You'd have to be crazy. Take this presenter—please.

Stories

If you want to add instant style to any presentation, just say these magic words: "Let me tell you a story…" Perks every audience right up, every time.

You have two choices here:

1. You can tell stories about other people.
2. You can tell stories about yourself.

If you choose to tell a story about someone other than yourself, it helps if the subject of the story is someone familiar to your audience. Suppose, for example, you want to convince an audience of science students that creativity thrives on chaos. You might consider telling them the following story:

The Advantages of a Messy Desk

You all know the story of how Sir Alexander Fleming discovered penicillin, don't you? It happened by accident when a speck of dust landed on an uncovered culture plate. Touring a modern research laboratory some years later, Fleming observed with interest the sterile, dust-free, air-conditioned environment in which the scientists worked. "What a pity you did not have a place like this to work in," said his guide. "Who can tell what you might have discovered in such surroundings!"

"Not penicillin," remarked Fleming with a smile.

Where do you find these illuminating anecdotes? We've included some ideas for you in Chapter 10, but you can also collect your own by reading—newspapers, magazines, biographies, and so forth. And here's another invaluable thing about anecdotes: Because they are true stories, they cannot be copyrighted. If you hear a wonderful anecdote from one speaker, it's yours for the retelling!

The stories you choose to include in your presentation will tell a lot about your preferred presentation style. If you are more a Professor than, say, an Entertainer, the stories you choose to tell will be more instructionally-focused than primarily amusing. A Preacher may use more inspirational people (Ghandi, Martin Luther King, Jr., Christ, Mohammed); an Orator may choose more inspirational events (the signing of the Declaration of Independence, the battle of the Alamo).

If you are a serious Professor who'd like to add a bit of humorous Entertainer to your next presentation, the best thing you can do is add a story or two about yourself—true stories, slightly (or magnificently!) embellished. It has been our experience that even the most inhibited, unanimated, most introverted presenters "come alive" when they are relating a story about something that actually happened to them. Why? Three reasons:

1. You don't need to rehearse. You just relate what you actually experienced.
2. You don't need to worry about delivering a punch line. You just relate what you actually experienced.
3. You don't need to "act" a certain way. You just relate what you actually experienced.

See how easy this is? Now, while you're "just relating what you actually experienced," two interesting things happen to your delivery style (WITHOUT YOU ACTUALLY THINKING ABOUT IT):

1. You relax, because you don't care so much about your stage presence anymore, you just want to share your story.
2. You start to move a little, gesture a little, because you *really* want to share this story. (And you're not thinking about your body so much, so you allow yourself to move naturally.)

If your story is a serious one ("What I learned from my three years as a foster parent of abused children"), your delivery style will, OF ITS OWN ACCORD, become more dynamic and dramatic. If it really happened to you, you won't be able to help conveying to your audience the depth of your own feelings.

If your story is a humorous one ("The time I put diesel fuel in my VW bus instead of regular gasoline"), you won't be able to HELP being funny. Indeed, telling a story about something you did in the past that now seems pretty dumb is the easiest way to add humor to a presentation.

Remember our earlier criteria for joke-telling? The same applies to stories:

1. *The story must be tried and true funny.*

A story about something funny that really happened to you is almost always funny, even if it was painful at the time. It can't help but become funny in the retelling because we human beings seem always to be able to look back at pain through the mist of exaggeration. Ellen, for example, tells a funny story about how she totaled her Volkswagen bug in a chile field when she was a teenager, woke up the next morning feeling miserable, heard a neighbor kid say, "Looks like your sister wrecked her car, huh?" and then cracked up as her little brother, Mike, replied, "No—she was in Africa on a safari and an elephant stepped on it!"

[Note: One lovely by-product of this technique is that you begin to cherish each painful event that happens to you as a potentially valuable story. You know that someday you (and perhaps hundreds of others) will look back at it and laugh.]

2. *The story must be actually relevant to a key point in your presentation.*

A story about yourself is easy to make relevant to a point in your presentation. (In the next chapter, we'll show you how to build such stories into your presentation design.) And it's such a wonderful humanizing technique—when you share a story about yourself with your audience, you're saying, "Hey—I know where you're coming from because I've been there, too." A personal story thus builds rapport and trust. If you think telling a funny story about yourself will make you look like a jerk, you're dead wrong; on the contrary, it will make you look like a human being. An *interesting* human being.

3. The story must be completely, 100% not offensive to any person on any basis whatsoever.

If you tell a story about yourself, you run practically no risk of offending anyone. Indeed, self-effacing humor is just about 100% offensive-proof. (Ask Rodney Dangerfield or Phyllis Diller.)

Make fun of yourself and you'll get laughs, not sneers.

Are you worried that you don't have any good personal stories to relate? Pshaw. We think you probably have lots. You just need some prodding to remember them. Use the topics below to jog your memory.

Sources for Personal Stories

- Your most embarrassing moments.
- Times you messed up.
- Times you had difficulty learning a new process or skill.
- Times you were in danger.
- Things about you that your husband/wife/children/friends really hate.
- Times you learned a hard lesson.
- The weirdest things you've ever seen.
- The funniest things that ever happened to you (or to a member of your family, a friend, someone you know, or a pet).
- The strangest teachers you ever had.
- The hardest things you've ever done.
- The funniest people you know.
- The people you love best.
- Family vacations.
- Your first car wreck.
- Your first day of school (any kind of school).
- Your first date.

And the list goes on—

Examples and Analogies

Do you want some magic words to liven up your presentation? Here are some you can use any time: "For example..."

If generalizations are the cause of boring presentations, then examples are the cure. Standup comics know this. They set up a comic bit with a generalization, and then punch in a specific example. For example (we're practicing what we're preaching here), in a routine he presented early in his career, George Carlin generalized about how the laid-back Sixties had quite an impact on the educational output of high school students. Then he got specific: "In one semester, students in shop class went from making zip guns to hash pipes." So the Sixties were an influential time? Oh, yeah, sure, I guess that's so, gee, so what else is new? Generalizations by themselves are boring. They are vague. They create no pictures in the listener's minds. But zip guns to hash pipes? Wow! Pictures! Everybody see those students in shop class? Any of you remember that you were one of those students? The laughter lies in the specific example.

It's easy to add lively examples to your presentation, no matter what your preferred presentation style. Just think of a point you want to make, and then say the magic words. For example (we're doing it again), in Ellen's writing classes she frequently points out that politically correct labels are fine to a certain extent, but we must be careful about taking things too far. (Now there's a generalization for you. Doesn't it just cry out for the magic words?) For example (of course), says Ellen, "I have a friend who thinks he's too short. He describes himself as *vertically challenged.*" Or how about this one? "I hear that we no longer refer to deceased people as *dead.* We now have to call them *living impaired.*"

A good example can explain your point by providing a context for new items or events. For example, if you are making a presentation on the benefits of a new office acquisition, you might say, "This new software will help us work more effectively. *For example,* we will no longer have to call up Excel to create charts; this program takes care of both computations and graphics."

For another example, suppose you want to convince your audience that your firm offers the best all-around service: "You can think of us as offering you a financial supermarket—one-stop shopping. *For example*, you would not have to make separate trips to your bank, your stockbroker, and your insurance agent."

For yet another example, you might wish to direct your audience's behavior by providing a model to be emulated: "Modern leaders could learn from historical figures. *For example*, George Washington was revered by his contemporaries because he did not seek power: He sought to serve."

For one last example, you can illuminate your point with examples that use key words or images: "We tend to describe the unfamiliar in terms of the familiar. *For example*, the first automobiles were called 'horseless carriages.' The first locomotives were called 'iron horses.'"

A type of hypothetical example is the analogy. Analogies work brilliantly because they always create pictures in your listeners' minds. Analogies compare two things that, on first glance, seem to be very different, but on closer inspection, actually have a lot in common. Analogies are a terrific technique to use in a presentation because they can be tailored to meet your audience's particular needs. If you are trying to describe a complicated new idea to a group of people, you will be must more persuasive if you can show them how the new idea is very similar to an old idea they already know. To do this, you have to create verbal pictures.

Some examples of analogies:

"Laws are spider webs through which the big flies pass and the little ones get caught." (Honore de Balzac, 1799-1850)

"Golf is a good walk spoiled." (Mark Twain)

Extended analogies are called parables. ("The kingdom of heaven is like...") The point of a parable is to lead your audience to realize gradually that they are actually listening to an analogy, not just a story. They get there when you end with, "And the moral of this story is…"

For example:

The Parable of the Boiled Frog

If you place a frog in a pot of boiling water, it will immediately try to scramble out. But if you place the frog in room temperature water, and don't scare it, the frog will stay put. Now, if the pot sits on a heat source, and if you gradually turn up the temperature, something very interesting happens. As the temperature rises, the frog will do nothing. In fact, the frog will become groggier and groggier, until it is unable to climb out of the pot. Though there is nothing restraining the frog, it will sit there and boil. Why? Because the frog's internal apparatus for sensing threats to survival is geared to sudden changes in its environment, not to slow, gradual changes.

And the moral of this story is—

If we act like frogs, we won't even realize it when our business goes under!

Visual Illustrations

If you're an Entertainer or a Preacher, you probably don't use visual illustrations very often—you prefer to use your body, your voice, and verbal pictures to illustrate your points. The great advantage of not relying on audio-visual aids (visual illustrations, things you can actually see) is that you never have to worry about them breaking down. (Entertainers, in particular, avoid anything that could possibly "upstage" themselves. They prefer to be the center of attention.)

We once attended a presentation on "New Technologies for Trainers," during which the presenter used a computer to project prepared visuals on a screen at least a hundred feet high in a ballroom holding a thousand people. The presentation started out fantastically: The visuals were indeed incredible, including both animation and sound. The audience was duly impressed. The speaker was highly gratified.

Suddenly, there on the screen a hundred feet high in front of the audience of a thousand people appeared the gigantic words: GENERAL PROTECTION FAULT. The entire program had shut itself down. For the next long ten minutes, the speaker fumbled about with various buttons, muttering, "Gee, I don't know why this is happening, this worked all right in rehearsal, wonder what will happen if I do this. . . ." The attendees began to dribble out of the ballroom, convinced that this miracle of modern technology couldn't hold a candle to a flip chart and marker.

So there is indeed a great weight lifted off your shoulders if you can avoid using any visual aids at all. But sometimes you can't get away with it: Not if you're making a presentation on new trends in the industry. (You're going to need some key word visuals.) Not if you're briefing the big bosses on reasons why your company needs to purchase a new veeblefetzer. (You're going to need printouts proving that the old veeblefetzer is no longer doing its job.) Indeed, if your presentation needs numbers, facts, comparisons, analyses, and the like, you're going to need some type of visual aid just to help your audience keep track of all the data.

Aha, we can hear you saying: So you agree that sometimes speakers HAVE to be boring, especially when they have to present lots of data. No, no, no. We stand by our original opinion. The presentation becomes boring only if you let the facts speak for themselves. When you use visual illustrations in a data-based presentation, the purpose of those visuals must be to *illustrate* the data, not just dump it.

One of the best books we know on the subject of constructing effective visual illustrations is Edward Tufte's *The Quantitative Display of Visual Information*. (See Chapter 10.) Tufte promotes "The Friendly Data Graphic," which he defines as a visual illustration designed carefully so that "it is particularly accessible and open to the eye, as if the designer had the viewer in mind at every turn while constructing the graphic." Specifically, Tufte deplores what he terms "chart junk," which is an ill-advised attempt by the speaker to load the graphic up with so much information that nothing can be learned from looking at it.

When it comes to visual illustrations, simple is best. And if you can make them funny, that's even better!

Quick Tip:
If you are not an Entertainer, if humor does not come easy to you, if you are not a comfortable joke-teller, the easiest way to add humor to your presentation is to SHOW something funny, like a cartoon or a humorous drawing. [Note: If you use a published cartoon, please be aware that you are using a copyrighted work and make every effort to get permission to use it.]

Here are a few ideas for some visual illustrations. Make sure you apply the humor criteria (1. Is it really funny? 2. Is it relevant to your objective? 3. Is it absolutely non-offensive?) before you use any of these. You can put these on a flip chart, or an overhead, or a slide, or a computer screen.

Every new project
goes through three phases:
1. It will not work;
2. It will cost too much;
3. I thought it was a good idea at the time.

The incredible is done here daily;
the impossible takes a little longer.

A little Murphy's Law for those in the military:

If the enemy is in range—so are you.

And a little Murphy's Law for all of us:

There's never enough time to do it right,
there's only enough time to do it twice.

One last reminder (if you're an experienced presenter, you should already know this) about using visual illustrations effectively, especially humorous illustrations:

Make sure they can be seen easily by everyone in the room. If they can't, don't use them. We don't care how funny they are; if your audience can't see them, they won't laugh. And if you have to explain it to them, they won't laugh either.

Tailoring Your Material for Your Audience

It should be no surprise to you that one size does NOT fit all when it comes to verbal and visual illustrations. What is meaningful to one audience will be nonsensical to another. What makes one audience fall off their chairs laughing will make another stare at you in stony silence. How do you know what to use?

It all depends on your audience, of course. In order to tailor your material to meet the expectations of your particular audience, you must do one of two things:

1. Choose material that you know will be familiar to your audience.

2. Adapt material to make it familiar to your audience.

If you know your audience well, if you're "one of them," and if you've already established a rapport with them, you can probably score big by using humorous material that makes your audience laugh at themselves.

Here's an exercise to show you how easy is to match the material to the audience. Simply decide which numbers (material) go with which letters (audiences).

Match the Material to the Audience Exercise

1. An accountant went to see an eye doctor who told the accountant to "cover one eye and read the bottom line." The accountant asked, "Before or after taxes?"

2. A bandit robbed a bank of $2,000 the other day and the teller tried to talk him into opening an IRA.

3. This situation reminds me of the Air Force fighter pilot who radioed the control tower: "The good news is that I'm making excellent time. The bad news is I'm lost."

4. A grocery store clerk, tired of his job, quit to become a law enforcement officer. After a few days, a friend asked him how he liked his new job. He said, "The pay and the hours aren't too good, but at least I now have a job where the customer is always wrong."

5. A utility company superintendent took two crews into the field to install poles. He gave each foreman the assignment and left to do other duties, saying he'd be back later to check on their work in progress. Upon his return, he asked one foreman how many poles the crew had installed.

First Foreman: "Twelve."

Second Foreman: "Two."

Superintendent: "Just two? The other crew installed twelve."

Second Foreman: "I know. But look how much they left sticking out of the ground."

A. Utility company workers

B. CPAs

C. Airline personnel

D. Law enforcement personnel

E. Banking personnel

[Note: It's easy to find material already pre-tailored and categorized. Just check out books such as *Speaker's Library of Business Stories, Anecdotes and Humor*, edited by Joe Griffith, and the others described in Chapter 10.]

To adapt existing material to match your audience, just choose jokes or stories that can be easily modified. For example, many so-called "light bulb" jokes can be easily tailored. Here's one:

"Q: How many _____ does it take to change a light bulb?

A: Five. One to change the bulb, and four to sit around and talk about how much better it was before the change."

Now all you have to do is fill in the space with any group that your audience would immediately recognize as being resistant to new ideas, new technologies, etc. You might choose managers, CEOs, union workers, boards of directors, and so forth. Nearly any group works with this joke.

[Note: Ellen, who lives in New Mexico, first heard this particular joke tailored this way: "How many Santa Feans does it take to change a light bulb?" (Same answer as above.) This version always gets a big laugh in Albuquerque. Mike doesn't think it would go over so well in Germany. He would have to change it to, "How many East Berliners does it take to change a light bulb?" (*Wie viele Ossis braucht man um eine Glühbirne zu wechseln? Fünf. Einer wechselt die Birne und vier unterhalten sich über wie schön es vor der Wende war.*)]

Here's another example of how to adapt existing material to fit your audience's expectations: Remember that joke we told you earlier, the one about the mathematician and the biologist who were scheduled to be executed on the same day? Ellen has used this same joke with training professionals at a conference; she merely substituted "an organizational development specialist" for the mathematician and "a technical skills trainer" for the biologist. Then all she had to do was have the "OD Specialist" propose to present a seminar on "New Studies in Chaos Theory and Its Impact on Organizational Subsystems" (or any such theoretical mumbo-jumbo). You can do the same: How about an architect and a construction worker? How about a physician and a nurse? How about a professor emeritus and a lecturer? How about a consultant and a supervisor?

Adapting Material Exercise

See how many different ways you can adapt the following to make it meaningful to a variety of audiences. (Remember to choose whether the main character should be a "he" or a "she.")

The time had come for a retiring _____ to turn over control of the company to his/her successor. After the standard speeches and banquets, the old _____ handed over two envelopes to his/her replacement. One envelope was marked number 1 and the other number 2.

His/her replacement asked, "What are these for?"

The old _____ replied, "When a crisis arises and you want to know what to do, open envelope number 1."

Sure enough, a few years later a crisis faced the new _____. He/she went into the privacy of his/her executive office and opened envelope number 1. It read, "Blame your predecessor."

Relieved, he/she followed the advice. Then a few years later another crisis developed and he/she found the second envelope. Looking for a solution to the problem, he/she opened the faded envelope, and the contents said, "Prepare two envelopes."

Design and Time
a Presentation with Style

What's the most sure-fire way to lull your audience into unconsciousness? Just do what your mother or father did to put you to sleep as a child: Read to them.

Oh, yes, we know that there are dynamic readers who can stir an audience's emotions with their ability to read dramatically, but—let's face it—most people do not fall into this category. On the contrary, most people tend to fall into a monotonous monotone. Most people tend to spend too much time looking at their written speech, rather than at their audience. Most people thus make reading a speech a custom devoutly to be avoided.

[Note: Many academic presenters fall into this category when they attempt to "read" a "paper" at an academic conference. For ways to deal with this particular speaking situation, see Chapter 8.]

So what is the alternative? Memorize your presentation so that you don't have to bend your head to read it? Well, yes, this could be a good thing to do IF YOU'RE A MASOCHIST. Do you want to cause yourself intense stage fright? Then you just try memorizing your presentation. You'll spend hours, maybe even days or weeks, worrying that you might forget your lines.

There's no point in driving yourself crazy trying to memorize a speech. Indeed, if you do try, you may wind up sounding artificial and "stagey." Rather, you want your audience to think that you are being completely spontaneous, off-the-cuff and on-the-mark. You want to come across as a person who knows exactly what he or she is talking about and exactly what objective he or she wants to achieve. You want to appear prepared and polished—and yet completely extemporaneous.

Can this really be done? Of course it can. Actors in the theater strive for this very effect. Stanislavsky, the "father" of modern acting techniques, called it "the illusion of the first time." You, like the actor, must spend significant time preparing and polishing your presentation, yet your audience should think that you are telling them things that you have never said before in quite that way. When you strive to create "the illusion of the first time" in your presentation, you unleash an incredible jolt of energy into your delivery.

But you don't want to just "blather," do you? You need SOMETHING to hold on to while all eyes are staring at you, waiting for you to enlighten them. What are your choices?

1. You could speak from notes on note cards. Lots of people use this method to good effect. The main problem with this technique is that you are pretty well stuck with the predetermined order of your cards. If an audience member interrupts or asks a question, you might get confused as to what card you should be speaking from next. Also, if you are holding note cards in your hands, you limit the number of hand gestures you can make. And what about this worst-case scenario: What do you do if you drop your cards just before you "go on," and you have no time to get them back in their correct order? The main problem with the note cards technique is that you can't see your entire presentation at a glance (and so figure out where exactly you are); you can only see the card that is currently on top.

2. You could speak from an outline. Again, many speakers use this method and it works well for them. But how useful is an outline going

to be if you've prepared a detailed, closely-scripted outline, in teeny-tiny type so you can fit it all on the page, and then you can't really see it very well from where you've placed it on the podium, so you have to pick it up to look at it, and now you've got something in your hands again limiting your gestures, and you look like you're reading a speech?

We think you need a better tool than note cards or an outline. We think you need a tool that will allow you to design a coherent presentation and then use that same design to speak from during the actual presentation. A tool that will allow you to change your mind, delete some points and add others (depending on your audience's responses), and basically go with the energy flow of your audience. A tool that will leave your hands free to gesture and your eyes free to make eye contact. A tool that will give you a visual representation of the shape of an effective presentation, so that you will always be aware of your "big picture" objective. And, finally, a tool that will allow you to time your presentation accurately.

The Presentation Diamond™

This tool is the Presentation Diamond™. Think about this for a minute. What sorts of qualities do you associate with a diamond?

It sparkles.

It's valuable.

It means "forever."

Aren't these the same qualities you want people to associate with your presentation? And consider the shape of the diamond: Points at the top and bottom, because you want to "tell 'em what you're going to tell 'em" at the start and "tell 'em what you told 'em" at the end. A wide space in the middle because here is where you're going to present the "meat" of your presentation, along with the material we talked about in Chapter 2. The diamond presents a shape for you to plot out each main point of your presentation, always keeping your objective clearly in mind (and in sight).

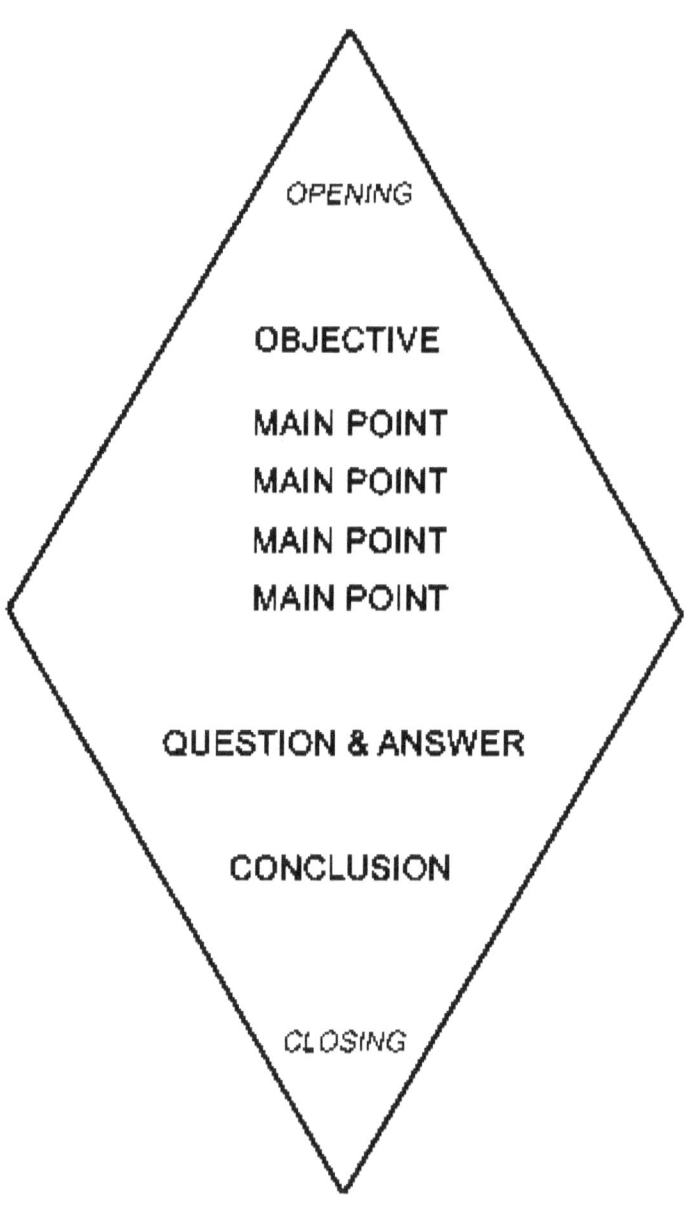

You see how easy it is to design a "well-shaped" presentation by using the Presentation Diamond™? At a glance, you can actually see the structure of your speech. All you have to do now is fill in the blanks.

We like to use small sticky notes to block out the first draft of a presentation. This method allows you to change your mind, without having to rewrite anything. Here's how to do it:

1. Write a few key words about your opening, your objective, each of your main points, and your closing on individual sticky notes. Don't write sentences: Just write a few words that will enable you to remember the whole thing later.
2. Place these notes in the appropriate places on the Presentation Diamond™.
3. Determine if they are in the best possible order (especially the main points).

For example, if we were going to make a presentation on, say, *Why Seaweed is Impractical for Stuffing Upholstery*, we might devise sticky notes like these:

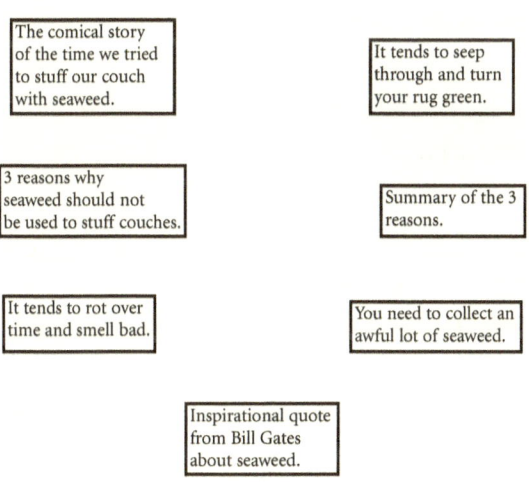

Now all we have to do is transfer these notes to the diamond. It should be fairly obvious which notes go where; the only decision we have left to make is in what order we should present the "reasons."

1. The odor problem.
2. The amount you need.
3. The seepage problem.

1. The amount you need.
2. The odor problem.
3. The seepage problem.

1. The seepage problem.
2. The odor problem.
2. The amount you need.

We will make our final decision based on our (vast) knowledge of the subject, as well as our understanding of what our audience will find most useful (depending on whether they're furniture upholsterers or deep sea divers).

You will notice that we assign separate sections at the top and the bottom of the Presentation Diamond™ for the "opening" and "closing" remarks. We believe that these should be listed separately from the objective and the summary because they perform such distinct functions in a presentation.

Openings

The first thing you say must get your audience's attention. It must quiet them down if they've been chatting; it must pump them up if they've been dozing. The first words out of your mouth will set the tone for your entire presentation; that's why so many people experience such severe stage fright in the first few minutes of a presentation. That is also why you must meticulously prepare those first few minutes.

> *Quick Tip:*
> Humor can work for your opening—if you're careful. If you're sure you can make a joke work, then by all means, start with one. If you're not sure, don't even try; go right to storytelling. Nothing works better for setting the tone and jazzing up the energy level than a good story, whether funny or sad, personal or anecdotal.

Here are some other options for openings:

- State an impressive fact.
  "One out of every six people in this room will die of cancer."
  "The federal government spent more money killing mosquitoes last year than you will earn in your lifetime."

- Ask the audience a question.
  [Note: Not a "test" question to a particular person. ("What is the traditional founding date of the city of Rome?") You don't want to alienate anyone in your audience right off the bat. Rhetorical questions asked of the entire group work best.]
  "How many of you have ever flown in a hot air balloon?"
  "Are you ever frustrated by delays in production caused by poor communication?"

- Give the audience a command. Ask them to *do* something: Write down an idea; fill out a survey; look at a visual aid or a handout.

- Hold up an object.

Just remember, whatever you do, that you must *prepare* this opening; you must not leave it to chance, or to triteness. ("Well, um, good evening, it's an honor to be here, blah, blah, blah....")

And, whatever, you do, NEVER OPEN WITH AN APOLOGY FOR SOMETHING IN YOUR CONTROL. We had the misfortune recently of being in the audience when the speaker began, "Well, I spent all week trying to come up with something to say tonight....")

Closings

Perhaps no section of a presentation is as important as the closing, since that's the last thing your audience will hear, and, therefore, the thing they are most apt to remember from your entire presentation. Closings must never be just "thrown away"—they must be prepared and practiced.

Here are some famous last lines:

"...that this government of the people, by the people, and for the people shall not perish from the earth." (Abraham Lincoln, *Gettysburg Address*)

"Though much is taken, much abides; and though
We are not now that strength which in old days
Moved earth and heaven, that which we are, we are:
One equal temper of heroic hearts,
Made weak by time and fate, but strong in will
To strive, to seek, to find, and not to yield."
                    (Alfred, Lord Tennyson, *Ulysses*)

"God doth not need
Either man's work or his own gifts. Who best
Bear his mild yoke, they serve him best. His state
Is kingly: thousands at his bidding speed,
And post o'er land and ocean without rest;
They also serve who only stand and wait."
                    (John Milton, *On His Blindness*)

"…free at last, free at last, great God Almighty, we are free at last."
(Rev. Martin Luther King, Jr.)
Powerful stuff, eh? The closing is not sometimes called the "climax" for nothing.

Quick Tip:
There are many useful ways to close a presentation, but we think two are best:
1. Quote a famous person;
2. Refer back to the story you told as your opening.

Using a quote from a famous person to close a presentation is a sure-fire technique for adding a final dash of polish and pizzazz. Plus, it's the easiest thing to do, since all you have to do is find a suitable quote and plug it in. The only really tricky part is that you must memorize this final quote, as it looks really tacky if you read it off a note card. (For this reason, we recommend that you stick to a *short* quotation.)

It's easy to find quotes; there are only about 9 zillion collections of quotes on the market, and the Internet is also a good source. (See Chapter 10 for more resources.) Just make certain that the quote you choose meets these three criteria:

1. The person you're quoting is familiar to your audience and also respected by them. (You don't want to quote from Sarah Somebodyorother. Or Adolf Hitler.)
2. The quote actually has some relevancy to the objective of your presentation.
3. The quote works for your personal presentation style.

We also think that a wonderful technique for closing is to refer to the story you began in your opening; this method reinforces the sense that your presentation has now come full circle. (We're confusing circles with diamonds here, but we think you get the picture anyway.) So if, for example, we begin our presentation with a humorous personal story about the time we tried to re-upholster our couch with seaweed, we could also end with that same story: "And so we swore that never again would we make all those trips to the sea for that smelly old seaweed. From now on, we're sticking to yogurt!" (Or something equally nonsensical, but you get the point.)

Presentation Objective

Immediately after your dynamic opening, you should clearly state your objective. Audiences like to know what they're getting into. (They also like to make sure that they're in the right room.) Don't make this section fancy, just get right to it: "Today I'm going present three reasons why crop circles are sure signs of alien visitation." You might even want to list the three (or four or more) main points right off, as a sort of overview for your audience. If you lean toward the professor style of presentation, you might also want to list your main points on a flip chart, or overhead. This audio-visual aid can then function as an agenda for your presentation, one that can be easily seen by both you and your audience.

Main Points

How many main points can you include in a presentation? That simply depends on how long you have to speak. If you've got 30 minutes, you can probably only include a few aspects of your objective; if you've got 3 hours, you can include a lot more.

This is where the sticky notes technique comes in handy: If you notice that you have more notes than will fit on your diamond, then you should take that as a warning that your presentation is getting much too complicated. Remember that your audience is going to try and remember what you say: They can only remember so much at one sitting. As Henry David Thoreau would say, "Simplify! Simplify!"

Question and Answer Section

You'll notice that the Presentation Diamond™ locates the Question and Answer period BEFORE the conclusion and the closing. There are two important reasons for this placement:

1. You want to be able to include any information in your conclusion that might have been raised during the question and answer period. If you do this, you will demonstrate to your audience that you were indeed listening to them. (This is particularly useful if the subject of your presentation is guaranteed to make a majority of audience members unhappy, like "Why the New Road Will Go Through Sacred Indian Land," or something.)

2. What if the last question you get is one you can't answer? What if the last thing the audience hears you say is, "I don't know. Oh, well, are there any other questions? No? Well, that's all I have, I guess…." Not a very confident closing.

When you formally conclude AFTER the Q&A, your presentation will come across as incredibly polished.

Presentation Conclusion

This section doesn't have to be fancy, either. Indeed, it can be a simple rehash of your objective, with a few observations thrown in that you collected during the Q&A. The point is to remind your audience of where they've been and what they've learned along the way. (This is also an incredibly useful technique if you're dealing with a hostile audience. The person who summarizes the discussion, no matter how heated or tense the discussion has become, stays in control by having the last word.)

Now let's talk about building timing into your presentation design.

Timing is Everything

There are 2 aspects of time that will significantly affect your presentation:

1. The time of day that you are presenting.
2. The amount of time you have been given to present.

Here's an easy test question for anyone who's ever spoken in public. What's the *worst* time of the day to make a presentation?

You know it: About 2:30 in the afternoon, an hour or so after lunch. Particularly if it's been a *heavy* lunch. This is the snooze hour. People's energy low-lights are on, and they will have trouble staying awake for even the most scintillating of speakers. If you prefer a Professor style of speaking, and you're planning to present a series of data-filled slides at 2:30 in the afternoon, save yourself the frustration—send a memo instead. At the worst possible time of the day to present, only Entertainers and Facilitators stand a decent chance of keeping their audiences awake.

Most other times of the day, it's a toss-up which style to use. Early morning audiences are sometimes a bit groggy from the night before and may need a little prodding from an Entertainer. Late afternoon groups are sometimes a bit burnt out, particularly if they've been listening to speakers all day (as at a conference), and may need a Preacher to pump them back up. After-dinner listeners can be tired from a long day, or jazzed a bit from a good meal and a spirit or two. (If they've had more than a couple of drinks, they may be extraordinarily receptive to an Entertainer with a joke or two to tell.) The best time to present, we think, is right before lunch, especially if the room is a bit on the chilly side. Experienced speakers know that the most attentive audience members are always cold and hungry! (And most receptive, then, to Professors.)

The point is that you need to take the time of day you're presenting into consideration as you plan and design your presentation. If you tune in to what your audience's energy level is likely to be at the time you're speaking, you will be much more likely to succeed at keeping their attention. Or at least you can get kudos for understanding their plight. There is a story told about George Bernard Shaw, the British playwright, who once wound up being the last speaker at the end of a long evening of droning presenters. When Shaw's turn to speak finally came, he merely stood up, looked sympathetically at his audience, and said, "Ladies and Gentlemen, the subject is not exhausted—but we are!" and sat back down. And received a standing ovation.

Sometimes it's definitely what you DON'T say that's important.

> *Let us have a reason for beginning and let our end be within due limits. For a speech that is wearisome only stirs up anger.*
>
> St. Jerome

Wise words from St. Jerome. There is no greater mortal sin in public speaking than going over your time limit. A rare audience will encourage you to go on. An atypical audience will tolerate your going over time. Most audiences will despise you for it. And they probably won't be paying much attention to what you're saying anyway, so why even try to drag it out?

"But I have so much to tell them," you lament. Of course you feel that way! You are the expert; they came here to hear you speak. Shouldn't they want to hear you speak indefinitely? Get serious. How much can they remember if you drone on and on? (You will remember that the goal of a successful presentation is to be *memorable*.)

> *The secret of boring people lies in telling them everything.*
>
> Voltaire

You don't want to tell them everything; you don't have time.

Once again the Presentation Diamond™ is a useful tool to help you not only design your presentation, but time its component parts, as well. It works like this:

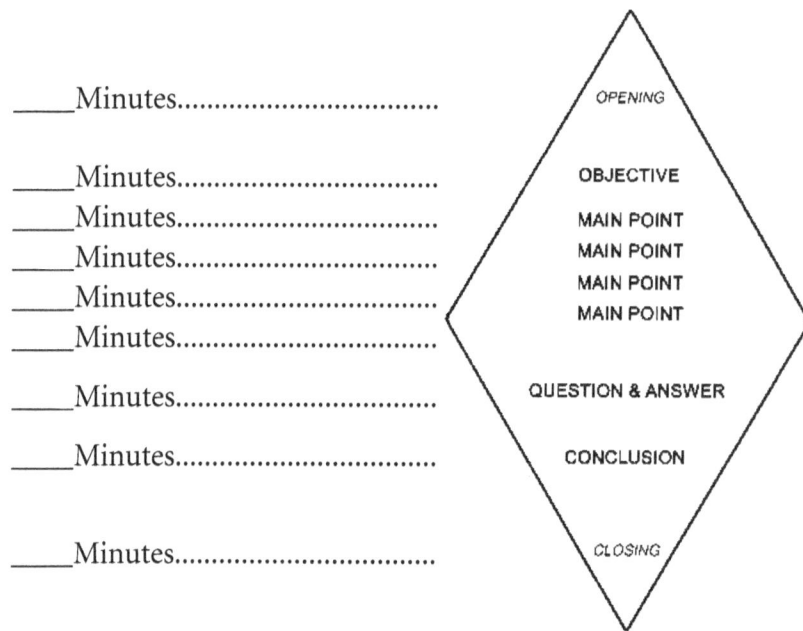

_____Minutes.................................. OPENING

_____Minutes.................................. OBJECTIVE

_____Minutes.................................. MAIN POINT

_____Minutes.................................. MAIN POINT

_____Minutes.................................. MAIN POINT

_____Minutes.................................. MAIN POINT

_____Minutes.................................. QUESTION & ANSWER

_____Minutes.................................. CONCLUSION

_____Minutes.................................. CLOSING

All you have to do is assign a certain amount of time to each section of your presentation, starting from the opening and the closing and working your way into the middle. Here's an example: Suppose you really do have to make a presentation on *Why Seaweed is Impractical for Stuffing Upholstery*, and you have been given 30 minutes to speak. You will time your presentation this way:

Timing the Opening and Closing

By our definition, these should be pretty short. In a 30-minute speech, you don't want to use up 20 minutes with an opening story. You figure that 2 minutes should be enough for a "wake 'em up" opening. Similarly, the closing should also be succinct. Remember, once you've said the magic words, "In conclusion—" to any audience, they're going to expect you to be a person of your word and ACTUALLY CON-CLUDE WITHIN A FEW MINUTES. So your closing better be concise. You decide 1 minute will be enough for a pithy final quote.

Timing the Objective

This is the point of the presentation, so you don't want to short-change it. On the other hand, the objective is also just the preview of coming attractions, so you don't want to spend too much time telling people what you're about to tell them. You figure that 3 minutes will be enough to lay out the agenda (the 3 reasons why seaweed won't work as upholstery stuffing).

Timing the Conclusion

This is actually a paraphrase of the objective ("And thus we can see that there are 3 reasons why seaweed..."), but may also include an observation or two picked up during the Q&A, so you want to give this section a teeny bit more time than you gave the objective. You assign 4 minutes to the conclusion.

Stop. Time for a math check. How much time do you have left? Only 20 minutes? (Makes you realize that a 30-minute presentation is very short, indeed.) Now you have to divvy those 20 minutes up among the remaining two sections: the main points of your presentation and the Q&A period.

Timing the Main Points and the Q&A Period

You have 20 minutes left, and 4 sections. You can distribute the time equally, 5 minutes per section. Or you can try to predict how much response you'll get during the Q&A, and then determine whether you need to add to or subtract from the time allotted to this section. If, for example, you know (from your audience analysis and presentation design) that your audience will be receptive to your objective, and may therefore have very few questions, you can limit the Q&A to 2 minutes, and distribute the 3 minutes left to the 3 main points, making each of them 6 minutes. If, on the other hand, you suspect that your audience may be skeptical about your objective, and may have a few questions, then you can limit the number of minutes for each main point, and allow more time for Q&A.

The point is that this system is eminently *flexible*: You can expand or contract the time for any section, depending on your time constraints and the needs of your audience. Plus, this system allows you to visibly plot out the timing of the entire presentation, so that you don't spend all your time on the opening, or forget to leave time for the Q&A.

Here's what your final Presentation Diamond™ with timing might look like:

Timing for a 30-minute presentation:

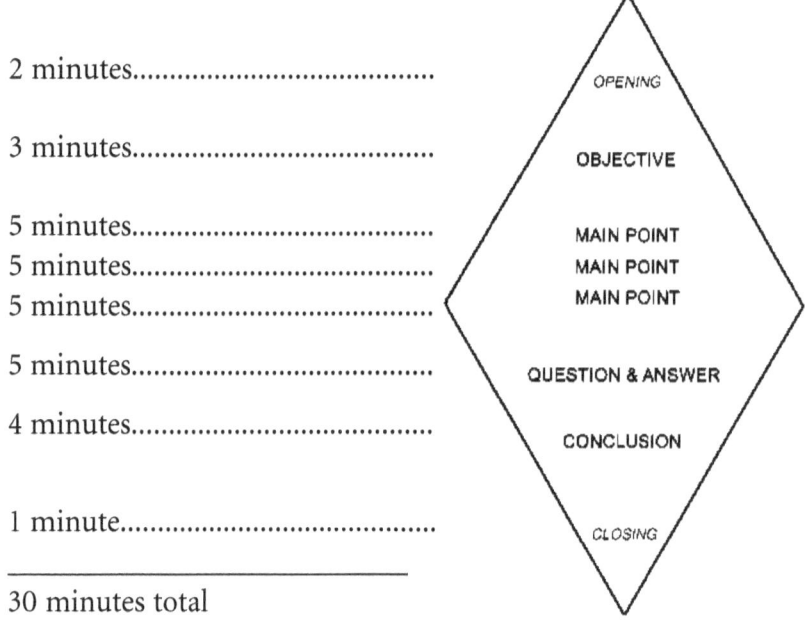

2 minutes...   OPENING

3 minutes...   OBJECTIVE

5 minutes...   MAIN POINT
5 minutes...   MAIN POINT
5 minutes...   MAIN POINT

5 minutes...   QUESTION & ANSWER

4 minutes...   CONCLUSION

1 minute...   CLOSING

_____

30 minutes total

Timing Worksheet

Subject of Presentation:
Audience:
Time of Day:

_____minutes....................................   OPENING

_____minutes....................................   OBJECTIVE

_____minutes....................................   MAIN POINT
_____minutes....................................   MAIN POINT
_____minutes....................................   MAIN POINT

_____minutes....................................   QUESTION & ANSWER

_____minutes....................................   CONCLUSION

_____minutes....................................   CLOSING

_____minutes total

Some Last Tips About Timing

What do you do if you've allotted a certain amount of time for the Q&A period, say 10 minutes or so, and no one asks any questions?

1. Maybe your audience is just shy. Sometimes you can prod them to start asking questions by asking yourself a question. Like this: "A question I am frequently asked is…." Sometimes that's all you need to do to get them to start participating.

[Warning: You can only use this technique ONCE, however. You'll look silly if you say, "ANOTHER question I am frequently asked is…." (If you're an Entertainer, however, this might get a laugh.)]

2. Maybe you've covered everything important, they really do have no questions, and they really want to get out of there. (Maybe it's happy hour.) In that case, forget the time allotment. Go right to your conclusion and your closing.

NO AUDIENCE IN HISTORY HAS EVER COMPLAINED THAT A SPEAKER CUT THE PRESENTATION A LITTLE SHORT.

On the other hand:

What do you do if you get too many questions during your Q&A period, so many that they push you over your time limit?

1. Take your cue from your audience and think about the situation you are speaking in. Are you the only speaker or the last speaker? Is the room going to be empty after your talk? Does it look as though the vast majority of your listeners are just hanging on your every word, desperate to hear what you're going to say next? Are they holding up lighters in the dark?

If so, then go ahead—speak as long as you (and they) like.

2. If not, then you get to say these magic words: "I'd like to answer all of your questions, but the time/the space/the situation/whatever does not allow me to do so. I'll tell you what—meet me out in the hall/in the room next door/in the closet/wherever and we'll continue our discussion there."

And then you get to do what every great performer strives to do with an audience: Leave 'em wanting more.

Prepare to Present

It takes me six weeks to prepare a good impromptu speech.
Mark Twain

In the theater, actors frequently rehearse for six weeks before the play opens. It doesn't take them six weeks to memorize their lines; they can do that in a couple of days. So what's taking them so long? What are they doing that they need six weeks to do it in?

They're GETTING IT READY FOR YOU, the audience. They're preparing their performances for public viewing. They're roughing it out, feeling their way, polishing their act, rehearsing their roles over and over again so that when you finally enter the theater you'll be completely bowled over by the spontaneity of it all. You'll remember we told you in Chapter 3 that Stanislavsky called this "the illusion of the first time." It's no illusion to the audience, of course: It IS their first time.

In this way speakers share much in common with actors. They rehearse a presentation to make it appear as though they were making it all up on the spot. (Actors have the added burden of attempting to make memorized dialogue seem improvised. Speakers, at least, can actually invent their lines on the spur of the moment.)

The problem for speakers is that sometimes they have six weeks to prepare; sometimes they have six minutes. Let's address both of these assumptions:

1. You have six weeks to prepare a presentation. What do you do?

Worry about it night and day. Obsess over how awful it's going to be, how stupid you're going to look, how quickly your career is going to end. Drive all your friends and family members nuts. Lose weight, lose hair, gain weight, lose hair, become a candidate for a coronary bypass. Be miserable for 42 days. Be frantic for 888 hours. Be catatonic for 53,280 minutes. Be certifiably insane for 3,196,800 seconds.

2. You have six minutes to prepare a presentation. What do you do?

Exactly the same as Number 1. But more quickly.

So it's a better idea to have no preparation time for a presentation? No, no, that's not what we mean at all. It is better to have lots of leisurely time to prepare for a presentation, but not if you spend all that time obsessing about *yourself*. The only productive way to spend your preparation time is to focus on your *audience*. And you do the same thing if you only have six minutes.

Let's face it: It's not about you, it's about *them*—their needs, their concerns. If there were no audience, there would be no presentation, just a lonely monologue.

Do you look all right? Are you dressed suitably for the occasion? Are you sure there's no toilet paper dragging off the end of your shoe and no taco sauce on your tie? Did you comb your hair? Then forget about yourself! YOU LOOK FINE! Just remember that the secret of great presenting is exactly what your mother always told you: "Stand up straight and don't fidget."

Quick Tip:

Do you want to overcome pre-presentation jitters? Do you suffer from stage fright? Do rabid butterflies invade your stomach before you go on? Here's the key to preventing the showtime shakes: STOP THINKING ABOUT YOURSELF AND FOCUS ALL YOUR ATTENTION ON YOUR AUDIENCE.

And you don't have to do this on a stage, or in a hall, or in front of your wife, husband, Aunt Bitsy, or your dog. You do it inside your own head.

We call it a "mind rehearsal." And you can do it for six weeks (intermittently) or six minutes (continuously). It looks like this:

Checklist for a Mind Rehearsal

- Who will attend the presentation? What kind of people will you be speaking to? (Are they, for example, salespeople, middle-managers, accountants, ex-cons, senior citizens?) Are they a homogeneous group, or are they a "mixed" audience? What concerns will they have?

- Why will they attend? Because they've been told to, or because they want to? (The answer to this question will determine how much motivation your audience will need.)

- What will they already know about your subject? Will they be totally unaware or completely misinformed? Will you have to "begin at the beginning?" Or will they already have a basic understanding and therefore need only further clarification? In other words, at what level of awareness are they?

- What "language" will the audience understand? Will they understand the "language" of computers? Or finance? Or management? Or engineering? If they do not speak the language, what "translations" will you have to make for them? (If your talk is about computers, can you assume that your audience will know what you mean when you tell them how to do a "cold reboot?" Will you have to say "get the computer up and running again" instead?)

- What will they want to learn from your presentation? All good speakers establish clear objectives for their presentation. But it's also important to consider what your audience's objectives might be. If their objective is different from yours, you have a problem to solve before the presentation. How will they respond to your objective? Will they be friendly and open-minded? Or will they be resistant and skeptical, perhaps even hostile? (Wouldn't you rather know this before the actual presentation?)

- What does your audience know about you? Do you already have credibility with them? Or will you have to establish credibility in the first few moments? Will the audience perceive you as "friend" or "foe"? (The answer to this will determine your opening comments.)

You can conduct a mind rehearsal in your car. You can do it in an elevator. You can do it walking down the hall. You can do it at the dentist, the hair stylist, the gym.

Obviously, if you have six weeks to prepare, you can really go into detail on some of these questions. You can thoroughly research your audience, learning their likes and dislikes, their concerns, their "hot buttons," their "language." You can then develop (using your Presentation Diamond™) stories, examples (OK, even jokes), or other humorous material to augment your presentation objective. Audiences love hearing about things familiar to them. Remember how easy it was for

Johnny Carson to get applause just by mentioning the name of a city or a state? It could work for you, too.

But not if you're completely self-conscious. "Do your homework," is still the best advice for a stage-fright-prone speaker. Learn all you can about THEM, and the rest will all fall into place. Guaranteed.

Before we leave this point: We also want to mention briefly why we think it's not a good idea for you to rehearse in front of a "fake" audience (your family, your friends, co-workers, etc.). Remember that your primary objective is to get a response of some sort from your audience. Your fake audience will not be able to give you an honest response because, in most cases, they will already be on your side, rooting for you.

For example:

Your presentation: Why the CEO of your company and the Board of Directors should approve your proposal for a company-wide system upgrade that will cost several million dollars.

Your fake audience: Your mom.

Your fake audience's response: "Oh, that was wonderful! Let's buy the new system right away. You are such a wonderful speaker. Are you hungry?"

OK, OK, we admit we're talking about extremes here. But we're serious when we say that a "mock" audience may not always give you useful feedback to help you predict how your "real" audience will react.

The one obvious exception is the fake audience who knows what your real audience will be like, and who can effectively improvise what responses such an audience might have. This kind of rehearsal can be especially helpful if you're going to be presenting a controversial subject to an audience who may be out to get you (or your company). Take your cue from the president of the United States. He or she would never dream of going to a press conference without rehearsing with staff members who have themselves rehearsed how to act just like members of the press. They ask the president the tough questions, so that he or she will not be thrown during the actual session.

If you're an employee of the State Highway Department in New Mexico, and your audience consists of members of the Navajo Nation, and the title of your presentation is, "Why the State is Planning to Build a Road through Sacred Indian Lands," they you'd BETTER rehearse with people who can pretend to be disgruntled Native Americans!

Our point is this: You can never prepare too much, as long as you're focusing on their needs, not on your own anxieties.

Quick Tip:
But let's say you still have some pre-presentation jitters, despite all your homework. Here's another tip for you: Set the stage for your audience before they arrive and you'll establish control over the situation and yourself.

Here's how it works:
1. Get to the space where you're going to present early. Maybe at least 30 minutes before your audience is due to arrive.
2. Walk around the space. Make yourself at home in it.
3. Set up your stuff. Unpack your AVs, boot up your laptop, test the overhead, whatever. Take possession of the space.
4. Re-arrange the furniture.
   a. Move the head table or podium (wherever you've placed your stuff) to a position where you can comfortably see and be seen by your audience.
   b. Re-position the audience's chairs (if physically possible). Move them forward, move them back. If they're in straight lines ("theater style"), move them into a "U" shape. If the audience will be sitting at tables, move the tables around a bit.

[Note: We understand that major furniture rearrangement might not be possible if you will be speaking to an audience of, say, 400 people in an actual theater or auditorium where the seats are bolted to the floor. Just move what you can.]

5. Once you have set the space up to your liking (now it's *your* space!), then go sit in one of the audience's seats. Sit there for a bit and imagine what it's going to be like to sit in this seat and watch the speaker up at the front of the room. Become a member of your own audience. Will you be able to see everything comfortably without craning your neck? How does the seat feel? How long will you be able to sit in that seat before you'll need to take a break? Then move to other seats, checking out the same responses from different angles.

This pre-speaking exercise is the best preparation we know, for it accomplishes two worthy goals:

1. It helps you overcome any butterflies you might be feeling by letting you take control of the space. So when the audience finally does arrive, you will be able to welcome them to *your* space, where *you* are the host.

2. It forces you to STOP THINKING ABOUT YOURSELF and spend the last few minutes before "showtime" thinking only about THEM: What they need, what they'll be seeing (and hearing*), what they'll be feeling. You will literally have sat for awhile in another's seat—always a morally admirable thing to do!

[*Note: For large audiences, you'll also need this time to rehearse with your microphone.]

But, you may well ask, what do I do if I can't manipulate the space before my audience arrives? What if I'm just one of a bevy of speakers, and have to follow someone who's already speaking in my space? (This happens frequently at conferences.)

Well, we admit that this is a little trickier to pull off. It's going to look very strange if you start messing around with the furniture while some other speaker is speaking. (If the speaker before you is really boring, of course, and hasn't read this book, the audience may actually appreciate your distraction.)

Here's a not-as-good, but acceptable, solution: Use a variation of the old "mind rehearsal" bit. Stand (or sit) in the back of the room while the other speaker is speaking. Look around you. Become one with the audience. Imagine that it's you they're looking at up there. Plan your strategy for when the other speaker has finished. Consider how you'll arrange your stuff, maneuver the podium, set up your laptop, etc. You can actually do everything you would normally do in the pre-presentation plan we described above—you just do it mentally instead of physically.

"Impromptu," indeed. It only takes a few minutes to create spontaneity!

Polish Your Technique

The premise of this chapter is that if you're going to be your own best audio-visual aid, then you'd better be interesting to look at and listen to. You'd better not speak in a monotone, or stare vacantly over the heads of your audience, or stand frozen in the "front fig leaf" position. You've got to speak distinctly and dramatically, and you've got to move around purposefully.

To improve your vocal skills, you need to concentrate on two aspects of your voice: *volume* and *variety*.

Can They Hear You?

If not, what's the point of being there at all? If you know your Latin, you know that the word *audience* comes from the Latin *audire*, meaning "to hear." Audiences hear speakers; audiences listen to speakers. You should be ashamed of yourself if one of your audience members has to yell, "Could you please speak up? We can't hear you back here."

The other extreme, much less common, is the speaker who speaks too loudly. (This may not be a problem for those in the back, but the people in front may be wincing.) The problem occurs when the speaker doesn't seem to know the difference between shouting and projecting: Excellent speakers PROJECT their voices to the back of the room, thus saving wear and tear on their own vocal chords as well as ensuring that all members of the audience can hear them comfortably. As renowned voice teacher Cicely Berry (*Voice and the Actor*) says, "Basically what is required is a voice which is big enough to share in whatever area you have to share it." (See Chapter 10.)

Here is an easy exercise you can do to discover the difference between shouting and projecting. (Turn on a tape recorder so you can play back and hear yourself.) First, try shouting. Shout out anything—your name, a quote, a nonsense phrase, whatever. Play this back and listen to yourself. Do you sound strident? Does your voice sound forced? Too high-pitched? Then do this: Put your hands on your diaphragm (the area on the front of your chest just under your breast bone). Now whisper the same phrase you shouted earlier. Whisper as loudly as you can and feel what happens to your diaphragm as you do so. Did you feel it tighten? You've just discovered your diaphragm.

Now tighten your diaphragm without saying anything. Keep your hands there so you can feel your diaphragm tighten. Relax. Tighten again. Relax. Now consciously tighten your diaphragm and speak at normal volume the same phrase you shouted earlier. Play back and listen to your voice. Does it sound louder? Stronger? More resonant?

If you practice consciously tightening your diaphragm when speaking, you will notice a gradual improvement in your vocal projection abilities. It won't happen overnight, but it will happen eventually if you practice. Remember, actors go through years of vocal training to develop their voices. (By the way, this exercise will also help you to overcome any "breathy" qualities in your voice.)

Here is one more exercise you can do by yourself to improve your vocal projection. As you drive in your car, turn on your radio (or tape player). Consciously tighten your diaphragm and sing along with your favorite songs. Don't just hum. Don't just mouth the words. Sing! Belt it out! (It doesn't matter if you can't carry a tune. You're in your car. Who's going to hear you?) Practice this exercise religiously and you'll eventually hear the difference in your speaking voice.

Are You a Hypnotist?

Does your voice convey a coma-inducing quality? There's nothing worse than a monotonous vocal delivery, especially after lunch or dinner. And suppose the audience is sitting through a slide show? Suppose the lights have been turned down and the video turned on? Do you hear that noise? Someone in the back is snoring.

[Quick story: Ellen actually saw this happen once. The speaker was presenting an after-a-heavy-lunch workshop, in a stuffy room, on the subject of "visioning." It wasn't too bad until the speaker, in a quiet, soothing voice, told everyone to CLOSE THEIR EYES as they "visioned." After only a few minutes, a muffled snort, then a full-blown *BBBBBRRRRRAAAAAYTTTTZZZZZ* could be heard from the back of the room. One of the participants had not only gone to sleep, but he had thrown his head back, opened his mouth wide, and was shaking the rafters with his snores. At least the rest of us were awake: We were laughing hysterically!]

Preachers, Orators, and Entertainers are usually adept at being able to vary their vocal delivery and add drama to their speech. Professors, on the other hand, are sometimes stereotyped as being the most boring to listen to. How many of you, for instance, remember an actual professor you had in college who droned on and on, never attempting to interest you in the subject? If your own preferred presentation style is that of a Professor, you may need a little more help in this area.

To add variety to your vocal delivery, you need to discover your range of "voices." Anyone can learn to be a decent mimic—you just have to listen carefully and practice. In your car, consciously mimic the voices you hear on the radio. At home, get out your tape recorder and listen to yourself as you practice a range of voices. You'll be amazed at how much variety you can add to your vocal delivery just by conscious practice and attentive listening.

Quick Tip:

To improve both your vocal volume and variety, tell stories during your presentation, especially stories about events that actually happened to you. We have found that even the most soft-spoken and monotonous-sounding speakers "come alive" when they tell a story about themselves. It's almost like you can't help it. Your vested interest in conveying your actual feelings to your audience invariably makes you speak up and with enthusiasm.

Don't Just Stand There—Move Something!

Your hands, your legs, your face, your feet, anything that will help create pictures of your points. Get out from behind that podium, and actually MOVE TOWARD YOUR AUDIENCE.

Quick Tip:

Consider the podium to be the place you say hello from after you've been introduced, the piece of furniture on which you place your diamond, and maybe the prop you lean against sometimes when you're listening to questions or comments from the audience. And that's it. Here's a fact that few inexperienced presenters know: YOU DON'T HAVE TO STAND BEHIND THE PODIUM JUST BECAUSE IT'S THERE. You won't break any laws if you walk to the side, or in front. Indeed, you'll establish much quicker rapport with your audience if you eliminate the "barrier" that the podium represents.

If you think you have to stay behind the podium because that's where the mike is, then ask for a remote microphone so you can walk around.

The object of your movement is to control the dynamics of the room's proxemics. Proxemics, as defined by the cultural anthropologist Edward T. Hall in his book, *The Hidden Dimension*, describes how people relate to each other spatially, and how this relationship affects our sense of territoriality. When you stand behind the podium, or sit behind a table, or preside over a dais, you are establishing your territory as separate from the space your audience inhabits. When you move into their space, you establish a sense of togetherness with your listeners.

[Note: You can also manipulate the proxemics of the space to deal with difficult audiences. See Chapter 7.]

Your main objective should always be to move where you can see all of your listeners and they can see you easily. (It's much easier to understand people if you can actually watch their mouths moving.) Do not let the furniture dictate where you will stand.

So while you're moving around the presentation space, manipulating the dynamics with your entire body, what are your hands doing? Are they locked in front of you ("front fig leaf" position) or behind ("reverse fig leaf")? Are they stuffed into your pockets? Are they playing with a pointer, or a marker, or a slide control? Are they toying with your necktie or your necklace? Are they twiddling your mustache? Or are they doing what they're supposed to—illustrating your main points with punctuation and emphasis?

Excellent presenters use gestures that add to, rather than distract from, the presentation. "Suit the action to the word, the word to the action," said Hamlet to the Players. Easy for Hamlet to say, since he wasn't standing in front of a skeptical group of first-level line managers about to endure an 8-hour seminar entitled, "A Total Quality Approach to Valuing Diversity and Managing Change while Thriving on Chaos." How is a presenter to know *which* gestures are suitable, which facial expressions appropriate?

You can't choreograph effective gestures—unless your goal is to come across as a Las Vegas lounge act. You've got to discover what works best for your particular presentation style.

Here are some descriptions of gestures and the presentation styles most likely to use them. Note also that we have included both the strengths (just enough) and the weaknesses (too much) of gesturing as you speak.

Presentation Style	Gestures	Strengths	Weaknesses
Preacher	Lots of large, sweeping, full arm movements, meant to embrace eternity.	Extremely dramatic. Can sweep an audience up with emotion.	Extremely dramatic. Will not be appropriate for less motivational talks.
Professor	More of a pointer: Point to the screen, point to the slide, point to the materials.	Good for punctuating points. Good for keeping listeners on track with materials.	Can get very repetitious and boring. Needs a little variety.
Entertainer	Lots of large, sweeping gestures, lots of facial flexibility.	Very interesting to watch, easy to picture the point being made.	Very tiring if overdone. Not at all appropriate for certain business applications (especially delivery of bad news).
Facilitator	Uses fewest gestures. Mostly writes on flip charts or the like, points to confirm assumptions.	Becomes almost unnoticeable, which may be what participants need if they're to drive the session themselves.	Becomes almost unnoticeable, which could lead to chaos if participants are not prepared to drive the session themselves.
Orator	Combines the Preacher and the Entertainer to a certain degree, but most emphasis is on vocal dexterity.	Useful for illustrating metaphorical flights of rhetoric.	Not useful if the gestures detract from the rhetoric.

If you really want to "see yourself as others see you," videotape yourself periodically and evaluate how you move in front of an audience. To concentrate solely on gestures and facial expressions (as well as general body movement), watch yourself on tape with the sound turned off. Then hit the fast forward scan button and watch yourself move at high speed: Any gestures that you make repeatedly will immediately be obvious, and you'll discover any "tics" you may not have been aware of before. Work on eliminating these tics for a month or two, and then videotape yourself again to check your progress.

Ron Hoff, author of *I Can See You Naked*, has developed another useful way for you to determine which are your natural gestures and which are artificial. "Stand in front of a full-length mirror [or video camera] with a large book in each hand," Hoff says. "Then, talk. At times, you'll raise one hand or the other in a gesture even though the books are heavy. Those are the real gestures. Save them. Eliminate all others. Those are *nervous* gestures."

How to Get a Standing Ovation

Whether or not you get a standing ovation will depend on two things:
1. The kind of presentation you are making;
2. Whether or not you "ask" for one.
Certain kinds of presentations will be more conducive to standing ovations than others:

Kind of Presentation	Conducive to Standing Ovation?
Briefing	Probably not. Audience is there to get information in a nutshell. Delivery will be second to content for them.
Sales Presentation	Definitely, if what you're selling is yourself and you are a political candidate (and the audience is planning to vote for you). Not so probable if you're selling health insurance options to new hires.
After-Dinner Speech	Only if you're *brilliant*. (Better be in top Entertainer form here; otherwise, you might want to slip out before they pick up their pieces of pie.)
Keynote Speech	Very probably, especially if you shine in your best Preacher/Entertainer/Orator mode.
Instructional Session	Probably not, but a real hoot when it happens.
Conference Presentation	Same as instructional, above.
Public Hearing	Most likely not. Too many skeptics in the audience?
Press Conference	Absolutely not. You'll be lucky if they don't eat you alive!

If you feel that the time is right, you can "ask" for a standing ovation by following these three steps:

1. Open your arms wide, hip-high, and say something like, "And now, in closing, I'd like to remind you what [some famous person] said about [my topic]."

2. As you say the last word, raise your arms slightly, palms held open and out from your sides, look up over their heads, and pause for a full beat.

3. Drop your hands to your sides, look down at the floor, and say, "Thank you."

They will burst into applause. Guaranteed.

Inter-Act with Your Audience

The most interesting part of making a presentation is the ultimate lack of control even the most prepared presenter may have over an actual audience. Oh, certainly, all the preparation we advised you to do in Chapter 4 will increase your chances of success dramatically, but—let's face it—there is no 100% guarantee that you'll have anticipated your audience's *every* reaction. Sometimes they'll just outright surprise you. This is what makes a live presentation so *interesting* (as in the Chinese curse, "May you live in *interesting* times").

[We've told you this before: If you can't take this particular "heat" of uncertainty, then get out the kitchen and just send the video.]

So the most exciting part of any presentation is the first few minutes, when you size up your audience and they size up you. If you want to start off on the right foot, you have to establish immediate *rapport* with them. Rapport means "relationship, especially one of mutual trust or emotional affinity" (*The American Heritage Dictionary*). It means being in synch with others, being in step with them, being on the same page, etc.

> *Quick Tip:*
> In the first few moments of your presentation,
> you've got to accomplish two important goals:
> 1. You've got to confirm that your prediction
>   of your audience's needs was accurate, and
>   that you did your homework thoroughly.
> 2. You've got to make them want to stay and
>   hear more.

[Note for #2: You don't necessarily have to make them *like* you. Suppose you're there to deliver bad news, for example. Suppose you're about to tell them that their stock values have plummeted since the last annual meeting. You can still make them want to hear you out, rather than stumble from the room rolling their eyes or yawning. Even if they hate you, they should want to hear what you have to say.]

If you're a true PRESENTER, not a mere reader, and if you've used the Presentation Diamond™ to organize your presentation, then you won't be tied to the podium or dragged down by your notes—you'll be ready to look at these people who have come to hear you, assess their needs accurately, and kick start your presentation into high gear.

All you need are

Three Foolproof Ways to Establish Immediate Rapport with Your Audience

1. Ask them a question. Four choices:
   a. A rhetorical question
      Example (for an audience in Orlando, Florida, attending a sales convention): "How many of you would rather be standing in line at Disneyworld than sitting in this room right now?"
   b. A survey question

Example (For an audience of public school teachers at an in-service workshop): "By a show of hands, how many of you have heard of John Rosamond and his theories about child-rearing?"

c. A factual question

Example: (For an audience of internal, lower-level employees): "How many senior vice presidents does it take to change a light bulb?"

d. An emotional question

Example: (For an internal audience faced with changes in company policy): "So how do you all feel so far about the company's new flex-time policy?"

2. Tell them a story.

a. About yourself

b. About someone else

3. Conduct an activity.

a. Play a game.

b. Break them into small groups, give them a problem to solve or a topic to analyze, and then ask for their responses.

Before we go into more detail about these techniques for establishing rapport, take a moment to think about which technique would work best under which circumstances. Also think about which technique would work best for which presentation style.

Establishing Rapport: Technique Analysis

Rapport Technique	When this would be a good idea	When this would not be a good idea	Which presentation style this would work best for
Ask a Rhetorical Question			
Ask a Survey Question			
Ask a Factual Question			
Ask an Emotional Question			
Tell a Story			
Play a Game			
Conduct a Small Group Discussion and Debriefing			

Let's see if you came up with the same conclusions as we did:

Ask a Rhetorical Question

This works well under most any conditions. After all, the objective of a rhetorical question is not to get an actual answer (as with a factual question). The aim is to just get a nonverbal response of some sort, like head-nodding or -shaking, smiling or groaning (depending on the question). It's just a reality check to see if they're with you from the get-go.

The only disadvantage might be if you have been completely incorrect in your pre-assessment of your audience's needs, to the extent that they surprise you by their response. For example, if you ask them—rhetorically—"Wasn't yesterday's announcement of the upcoming layoffs a really crummy way to start the week?" and, instead of wry grimaces and dejected-but-resigned nods, you get startled glares and open-mouthed shock (because they hadn't yet heard about the layoffs), then obviously you're in trouble. Boy, did you pick the wrong way to begin!

Any of the five presentation styles can use this technique effectively. It comes most naturally, perhaps, to Entertainers, who (like standup comics) like to start with a question to get the energy level up. ("Hey, how are you all doing today? Is everybody having a good time?") It's also a proven technique for Facilitators, who also like to begin with an immediate (if only nonverbal) response from the audience, setting the stage for the give-and-take to come. Orators likewise make frequent use of the rhetorical question. (Remember, "Are you better off now than you were 4 years before?") Preachers and Professors are less inclined to start with a rhetorical question, anxious as they usually are to get right into the material they are there to present. So it would be a good idea for these 2 styles to try a rhetorical question once in a while, and see how it feels to make a quick bridge from speaker to audience. [Note: You can't read a rhetorical question and make it work; it absolutely has to appear to be spontaneous.]

Ask a Survey Question

This is an excellent way to confirm your predictions of your audience's level of awareness about your topic. If, for example, you ask your audience of teachers if they know who John Rosamond is, and if they all (or most all) say they do know of him, then you have confirmed that you will not have to go into too great detail about Rosamond's background and beliefs. If most of them do not know him, then you will have to backtrack to fill in their lack of knowledge. There really is no direct disadvantage to this technique: Any response you get from your audience will be useful information, and you can then adjust your presentation accordingly.

Most presentation styles are comfortable with this technique, especially Orators, who like to see a "show of hands" as often as possible. (Any politician comes to mind.) Preachers are probably the least comfortable asking survey questions, because they are usually more concerned with promoting their own beliefs than encouraging diverse opinions. A Preacher who might ask, for example, "How many of you in this audience feel strongly that the moral fiber of our country is seriously unraveling?" might feel much too disconcerted if a portion (or, heaven forbid, a majority!) of the audience members do NOT feel that way. Still, it would be useful information for the Preacher to learn at the start of the presentation, rather than at the end!

Ask a Factual Question

This can be attention-getting, all right, but it can also come across like a "test" question that can put your audience on the defensive. [We are reminded of an old Bob Newhart Show episode, where the speaker finished speaking on some now-forgotten, but serious, topic, then asked if there were any questions. From the back of the room, one of the "Darryls" shot his hand up and asked, "Where is the Rock of Gibralter?"] It's more effective if you ask a "startling" factual question, and then answer it yourself. ("How much money has the United States spent so far to put the Space Shuttle into orbit?" "How many children were killed by their own parents in the United States last year?" "Which country in the world produces the greatest number of automobile engines?")

Professors obviously take to this technique enthusiastically, since they perceive it as following the Socratic method of instruction. (Socrates, you will remember, taught his students by means of a series of gradually more and more pointed questions.) If you're conducting a training session, you might want to ask factual questions by way of review on the morning of the second day of training. (If you're an Entertainer, you'll probably want to turn this technique into a game, some sort of adaptation of "Jeopardy!") Facilitators usually shy away from this technique, but they could consider using it a bit in some sort of summary session.

Ask an Emotional Question

If you need to assess the mood of your particular audience, an emotional question is an effective way to start. Asking "How many of you feel…" about anything important to them shows immediately that you are sincerely interested in their reactions to the topic at hand. The major disadvantage of this technique is that it can stir up a crowd if they're already feeling pretty emotional in the first place. For instance, "How do you all feel about those jerks we've got in upper management?" may not be the best way to start if you're hoping for an objective, balanced discussion of the company's policies. But if you teach, say, a grammar class (as Ellen does), you might ask, "How many of you feel intimidated by all the rules of grammar?" The benefit here is that those who do feel intimidated will immediately feel better when they see that they're not alone.

Preachers, we shouldn't even have to tell you, love this technique. Since they're often going for an emotional response to their talk, they prefer to stir the feelings up as quickly as they can. Orators likewise have a tendency to begin a presentation with a heart-string-tugging question. Sales presenters (usually a combination of Preachers and Orators) like to begin by asking immediately, "How many of you feel that your current job is taking you nowhere? How many of you would feel happy if you could take home at least three times the salary you're making now?" "We don't sell products," you'll hear the sales presenter say to the audience, "We sell emotion!"

(Maybe a serious Professor style could use a little of this technique to get students to "buy in to" the learning process. After all, which is the harder sell—a product or an idea?)

Tell a Personal Story

"Let me begin by telling you a story." Most audiences perk right up when they hear this. After all, the art of storytelling is as old as the history of humankind. Long before MTV and CNN, there were storytellers, providing entertainment and instruction to audiences eager to hear. You establish immediate rapport easily when you start with this technique. We can't think of any situation where a story wouldn't be a great way to start.

"Do you all know the story of how Sir Alexander Fleming discovered penicillin?" [If you don't, go back to Chapter 2; it's in there.] What a dynamic way to begin a presentation on, say, the mysterious ways of creativity. Audiences are usually mesmerized by such stories: stories about famous people who failed a whole bunch of times before they finally succeeded (Abraham Lincoln comes to mind); stories about serendipitous discoveries (Sir Alexander Fleming); stories about creative techniques (Albert Einstein shaving); stories about what makes us all human ("Those Amazing Amoebas" or "The Story of the Stressed-Out Rats," in Chapter 10).

Entertainers obviously love this technique. Egotists that they tend to be ("Is everyone looking at me?"), they enjoy talking about themselves to make a point. (They have to be careful, remember, not to just tell stories for the sake of the story, but to illustrate a presentation objective.) Orators may sometimes use themselves as the basis of an instructional story, but (like Preachers and Professors) they usually prefer to tell stories about other people. Orators love stories too, because inspirational anecdotes can move an audience to acceptance. Preachers love them because they are the foundation of belief: What are the Bible, the Koran, the Torah, the Tao but collections of inspirational stories? And how many of the world's revered prophets (Jesus, Mohammed, Confucius, etc.) spoke in parables (stories with a moral) when communicating with their disciples? Facilitators rarely tell stories, but should consider doing so now and then, just to liven up the joint. Personal stories are just too good as instructional tools to ignore.

Play a Game

If you choose to involve the audience from the start in some sort of interactive exercise, such as a game, be sure you've done your homework thoroughly. People attending a session on "Why the company is going to cut back on health care benefits" will probably not be too enthused at the thought of playing a quick round of "Icebreaker Bingo" or "Twister." But if you're a trainer, an activity can be an energizing way to start your session. If you're an after-dinner speaker, some sort of game that people can play sitting at tables and eating dessert could wake everyone up and get them listening again. [See Chapter 10 for sources for interactive exercises.]

Facilitators shine using this technique. After all, their primary objective is to involve the audience in the proceedings as quickly as possible, and a game most always gets participants participating right from the start. Entertainers also like games, as long as they can shine as the Master of Ceremonies. It's a good idea for an Entertainer to relinquish the spotlight once in a while, and an exercise will do just that. Professors can do likewise, using a game as an instructional self-learning device. A game is certainly a dynamic break from a static lecture!

An interactive activity is most anxiety-producing for Preachers and Orators, who usually need to feel in complete control of the presentation. It would be indeed good for their presenter souls, then, to take that risk once in a while, as the situation allows.

Conduct a Small Group Discussion and Debriefing

Logistics are going to play a large part in whether you have any choice at all about using this technique. If you are presenting in a large auditorium, for example, with "theater-style" seating, it's going to be very difficult for people to rearrange themselves comfortably into small groups. But if you are in a large ballroom and people are seated at round tables, then you shouldn't have any problem making this technique work. [If you want more details on how to do it, you need to attend one of Bob Pike's Creative Training Techniques seminars. For more info, see Chapter 10.]

Facilitators rely on this technique because, like a game, a small-group activity allows the participants to learn from each other, rather than from the presenter alone. But it's not always a good idea to rely on self-teaching. Suppose, for example, that your audience has come to your session to learn "How to Use the Latest Version of the Latest Computer Operating System" and they're all people who have just purchased their first computer. If you put them into small groups, they're probably just going to stare helplessly at each other. We think the Professor would be a much more appropriate style and the lecture a much more appropriate format for this group.

Entertainers probably need to use this technique much more frequently than they do. Given the Entertainers' natural proclivity to hog the spotlight, it's good for them to stop doing all the talking and let others speak now and then. Professors should do likewise, when the topic is not completely factual or skill-based, but one that requires analysis and evaluation. (If your topic is "Three Ways to Change a Light Bulb," you should lecture. If your topic is "Light Bulb Changing as an Indicator of the Moral Turpitude of Our Society," then you should probably include a small-group discussion activity.)

Preachers, of course, do not employ this technique very often. ("Now let's get into small groups and discuss whether my company's veeblefetzer is more productive that our competitor's veeblefetzer.") Nor do

Orators. ("Now let's get into small groups and discuss whether you're going to vote for me in the next election.") But maybe they should think about it once in a while.

Keep the Rapport Going

So much for getting started. How do you keep the rapport going throughout the remainder of your presentation? Well, for one thing, you just keep repeating whatever technique seems to be working best, both for your own particular style and for your audience. Ask questions periodically for feedback, tell a story again, break them up into small groups for a few minutes, whatever. It will all depend on how much time you have to present, the circumstances under which you're presenting, your audience's reactions, and your own comfort level with each technique. Mainly you take your cue from them: If they seem to be interested, wide awake, responsive, and enthusiastic, well, hey—whatever you're doing, keep doing it!

If you've assigned a formal Question and Answer Period to your presentation design, you can keep the rapport going even if you find yourself being asked "tough" questions. All you have to do is practice the following

5 Techniques for Effectively Managing the Q&A:

1. Remember to place the Q&A on your Presentation Diamond™ *before* the Conclusion. (See Chapter 3.) You want the "last words" to always be yours.

2. Ask for questions and wait. (This is so hard for Entertainers to do—they hate "dead air.") Some audiences might not be warmed up yet and need a second or two to respond. Look around the room, making brief eye contact with as many people as possible. If you see someone who looks like they're about to speak, give them a little nod of encouragement. Let your audience know that it's safe for them to speak up. (Of

course, if you're a government official who's just been accused of having a scandalous affair with an intern, and your audience consists of members of the press, you probably won't have to encourage them to speak up.)

3. While someone is asking a question, REALLY LISTEN TO IT. Focus all your attention on the question; move closer to the questioner to make sure that you hear it correctly. Make the questioner feel that he or she is the only person in the room.

4. Once you've heard the question, paraphrase it for the rest of the audience. A paraphrase has several benefits:

    a. It ensures that all members of the audience actually hear the question.

    b. It allows you to confirm that you understood the question. (The questioner should indicate "yes" or "no" after your paraphrase.)

    c. It may defuse any hostility the questioner may have toward you, since you will both have to "agree" on what the question is.

    d. It buys you time while you try to figure out an answer.

5. As you begin to answer the question, make eye contact with the questioner for a few moments, then break away and make eye contact with the entire audience. Remember that individuals ask the questions, but the *group* needs the answers. Don't let the situation become "one to one." Keep it "one to many."

When you are finished answering the question, make eye contact with the questioner again and say, "Does that answer your question?" If the questioner says no, then try the whole process again. Then open it up again to the audience as a whole.

[For more info on what to do if things get out of hand in a Q&A, see Chapter 7.]

Whether you get real questions or questions-disguised-as-threats ("When are you idiots going to get your act together?"), remember that when people ask questions, they're involved. You know where you stand with these people, because they are truly *participants*. Cherish them.

Stay in Character

We'd like to start this chapter with a survey question:

How many of you reading this book have ever participated in a live stage performance?

(We notice that quite a few hands have gone up.)

Another question:

We don't necessarily mean that you acted the part of Hamlet or Blanche du Bois. Any live performance will do, like, for example, the Pumpkin in the Fifth Grade Thanksgiving Pageant.

(Ah, lots more hands are now raised.)

We are not surprised. It's quite natural for those who have been bitten by the "theater bug," no matter how superficially, to be intrigued by the chance to stand up in front of a group of people and emote. After all, an audience is an audience, whether they have paid to see you stab Polonius through the arras, or they have stopped by to hear you explain the new corporate health benefits. When you stand up to speak, all eyes are on you, you are on the stage, and you are "on."

In the theater, the actor on stage portrays a character. This character may be quite different from the actor's own personality. (Indeed, we usually consider it a hallmark of expertise that an actor can play many extremely different characters convincingly.) On the other hand, actors who play characters very close to their own personalities are referred to in theater jargon as "type cast." As we established in

Chapter 1, your presenter style should be closely tied to your own personality type, so that you will feel more comfortable on stage. A presenter should not "play against type," as an actor might. You want to work from your strength.

But whether you are a corporate CEO delivering a new-hire orientation welcome, a health care practitioner presenting an instructional lecture on how to implement a disease management program, or a law enforcement official telling an audience of teenagers how to avoid getting mixed up with gangs, you all share something in common with the actor portraying a dramatic figure invented by a playwright—if something goes wrong during the performance, you have to STAY IN CHARACTER.

If you've ever been in a live theater production (and we know many of you have), then you probably have many stories to tell about "the night that this terrible thing happened, which wasn't at all funny at the time, but is hysterical now in the retelling of it." Indeed, this is the joy of live theater: You never know when you're going to get to see someone mess up! Actors frequently miss their cues, drop their lines, forget their props, or go blank. Phones on stage don't ring when they're supposed to, or (worst-case scenario) they ring when they're NOT supposed to. Doors on stage stick when you try to open them, or they just slowly open by themselves in the middle of a scene. Stage walls (called "flats") fall on actors. Actors' fake mustaches fall off. A live production can be a veritable melange of mistakes!

What can go wrong during a live presentation? Overhead projectors won't project (and the spare bulb will always be missing). Flip charts will run out of paper, or collapse. Markers will be all dried out (or else you'll use permanent markers on the white board by mistake, then not be able to erase what you've written). The room will be too hot or too cold (and your participants will hold you personally responsible for this). Best yet, during your painstakingly produced Power Point presentation, you'll hit the wrong key on the computer and crash the whole system. (Is there anyone reading this that this hasn't happened to?)

Whether your wig falls off or your flip chart falls flat, you and the actor have got to do the same thing: STAY IN CHARACTER.

For the stage actor, staying in character means reacting to any unforeseen event as the character would. For example, if you are playing Hamlet, and one of the walls of the "castle" falls on you during your soliloquy, you are not supposed to freak out, shout a modern obscenity, or (worst of all) turn to the audience and apologize. As Hamlet, you have only two options: 1. Ignore the whole thing and go on as though it never happened; 2. Ad-lib a response in character. ("Ah, methinks something is indeed rotten in the state of Denmark!")

If you're performing in a serious drama (can't get much more serious than *Hamlet*), it's best to just ignore the problem; a humorous ad-lib will seriously undercut the play's tragic tone. If you're in a comedy, you can choose the ad-lib option more often; after all, it really doesn't matter if the audience is laughing *with* you or *at* you, as long as they're laughing, period.

For presenters, the choice depends upon your preferred presentation style. It makes sense, doesn't it? Entertainers are most likely to go for a gag response when something goes wrong during the presentation. They've probably set up a fairly relaxed, light-hearted tone to begin with, so their audiences will be expecting some sort of witty remark when a mishap occurs. Facilitators, as well, may be able to use a little off-the-cuff humor, since they've probably already set up an informal atmosphere. (Facilitators would also be most likely to encourage members of the audience to react to the problem: "So what do YOU do when this happens to you?")

For Professors, Preachers, and Orators, it's a little trickier. We've already established that jokes don't come easily to these styles; witty ad-libs don't either. We think that the extreme versions of these three styles would much prefer to just keep going, stay professional, get back on track, and ignore the whole thing. Depending on the subject, their audience would probably prefer that they just get on with it, too.

On the other hand, maybe an unexpected quip from a hitherto staid Professor might bring down the house and be just the shot of adrenalin a lethargic audience needs. It's not always an easy call; you have to do what feels right to you.

What follows is a list of potential speaking problems (from Lilly Walters' *What to Say When*), followed by a potentially humorous remark. You decide which of the five styles would be most comfortable using which remarks, and which would rather just ignore the problem and go on. (And don't forget to indicate which ones you personally would use.)

Presentation Problem	Witty/Humorous Remark	Presentation Style
Your microphone shrieks horrendously.	"OK, there you have the note! Let's all sing!"	
Your microphone goes dead.	"How many of you in the back of the room read lips?"	
The electricity goes out.	"It appears that I have to shed more light on the subject."	
The overhead projector won't work.	"This must be one of those old wood-burning models."	
A piece of equipment breaks.	"This item just took a break, so why don't we take one, too?"	
You can't find one of your audio visuals.	"I had it here just a month ago."	
An audience member's phone or pager beeps.	"If that's for me, tell them I'm not here."	

We think you'll agree that most of these remarks would be suitable only for you high-Entertainer styles. For the rest of you, just keep your cool, ignore the problem, and stay in character.

It's frustrating, we know, to deal with inanimate objects that mess us up in the middle of a presentation. But they are, after all, *inanimate*—they just fail to do the job they were supposed to do (turn on, turn off, just work, darn it!). They don't stare at you resentfully, or fall asleep during your most important point, or laugh inappropriately, or talk to their neighbors, or leave early, or arrive late, or ask you questions you don't understand or can't answer. These kinds of problems are reserved for the *animate* objects in your presentation—the members of your audience.

Now here's where all your homework will really pay off. Nine times out of ten, you'll be able to anticipate any problems that might come up among the members of your audience. Ellen, for example, teaches a basic grammar class. Every once in a while an adept writer will actually attend the class, just to get updates or clarifications. But Ellen knows from long experience that most of her attendees will be there because they were sent there. Most will be folks who never liked English in grade and high school, who barely passed their courses, and who had hoped never to have to take another English class again. And so they tend not to be terribly happy campers at the start of the class. Ellen knows this, so she is never surprised by sullen faces and recalcitrant initial responses. She just schedules time at the beginning to calm them down and jazz them up. (This is the rapport we were talking about in Chapter 6.)

Still, no matter how thoroughly you prepare, specific members of your audience will find ways to drive you nuts. Thus, the presenter with style must be ready at any time to employ any one of a number of ways to tame misbehaving audience members. Taking a tip from England's favorite dog trainer, Barbara Woodhouse, your goal must be

No Bad Audiences!

Here are the top ten most annoying things audience members do to presenters:

1. They arrive late for the presentation (or leave early).
2. They start up a conversation with their neighbors.
3. They fall asleep during the most important part of the presentation.
4. Their beeper/phone goes off, loudly.
5. They won't ask any questions during the Q&A.
6. They ask questions you don't know the answer to.
7. They ask complicated, multi-part questions.
8. They disagree with you out loud.
9. They get so excited about your point that you can't get their attention back.
10. They are the wrong audience for your presentation.

See if you can determine how each of the five Presentation Styles might respond to these annoying behaviors:

Annoying Behavior	Preacher's Response	Entertainer's Response	Orator's Response	Facilitator's Response	Professor's Response
Arrive late; leave early					
Talk to neighbor					
Fall asleep					
Beeper/Phone					
No questions					
Questions you can't answer					
Complicated questions					
Disagree vocally					
Distracted					
Wrong Audience					

So how did you do? Did you remember to require each style to stay in character? This is especially important when the audience is annoying, aggravating, or upsetting in any way. Your first reaction may be to annoy them back, to irritate them as much as they're irritating you. You may be (justifiably) tempted to try some of the following retorts standup comics use when they get heckled in a comedy club:

- If the heckler interrupts you with a mild crack, cup your hand around the microphone and say, "Security, table twelve. We have a live one."
- If someone shouts at you incoherently from the back of the room, try "Sir, would you slur that a little louder," or "Just feel free to shout out meaningless crap anytime you feel like it, ma'am."
- If the heckler is particularly insistent, appeal to the rest of the audience: "Ladies and gentlemen, we live in the greatest nation in the world and what makes it so great is that it is a democracy. That means we all get to vote. So I want each of you to vote right now. By your applause, how many of you think this woman should JUST SHUT UP!"

These are great, huh? If you're a standup comic, you can use these as often as you like. You can enjoy the thrill of squashing a heckler like a bug, and of asserting once and for all your power over the audience.

But you're not a standup comic; you are a presenter, and you can't use any of these. Sorry. Your job is to bring a message to your audience. If you make fun of individual participants, you'll alienate them. They won't learn anything or be convinced of anything. Plus, you'll probably alienate the rest of the audience as well. Then no one will learn or be convinced.

Let's see how your analysis of the most appropriate responses for each style corresponds to ours.

1. An audience member arrives late or leaves early.

The first question to ask yourself, no matter what style you favor, is this: "Is this person distracting the audience by his/her early/late arrival?" If the answer is no, then the best response for all five styles is the same: Just ignore them. Or give them a slight nod to acknowledge their presence, and just go on with what you were saying. Check with your Presentation Diamond™ if you go blank for a few nanoseconds; you'll be back on track in no time.

Most people who arrive late will be very courteous about tip-toeing in. They don't want to be embarrassed, either, by everybody in the room staring at them as they enter. Same with leaving early. Most people who are going to do this will probably have chosen to sit in the back of the room anyway, and they'll just slide on out quietly.

Rarely will someone make a big production number of their movements, unless they're forced to by room constraints, like maybe they have to cross right in front of the speaker to get to their seat, can't be helped. Entertainers can handle this distraction quite courteously, with a smile and a gesture: "Welcome! We were saving this seat just for you!" Facilitators probably have the audience divided up into small groups by now, anyway, so they just go over to any newcomers and lead them to a seat without disturbing anybody. Professors can just draw the audience's attention away from the late arrival by asking the group to look at a slide, or the flip chart, or a handout.

The two styles who have the most difficulty with this kind of interruption are the Orators and the Preachers. Since both styles depend so heavily on audience concentration (on the words with Orators, on the emotion with Preachers), the smallest distraction can be difficult for them to deal with. If one of these is your preferred style, you can try a little humor ("Come on in, it's not too late to be saved!" or, as someone leaves the room, "There goes another satisfied customer!"), but mainly you'll need to just ride with the interruption until the audience comes back to you. Pump up the volume a bit, go right into a story, and you should have them back with you in no time.

2. A few audience members start talking to each other during your presentation.

Don't be too hasty to react to this situation. After all, they may be avidly discussing some point you just made. Let them chat for a few minutes, as long as they don't really seem to be distracting any of the audience members around them. Just keep tabs on them.

Then, if they seem to be going on for too long, and if people sitting near them become distracted, you can try a couple of different tactics. Entertainers can put on their best "Miss Thistlebottom-English-Teacher voice" and prance toward the talkers, saying, "All right now, you two. Is what you're talking about so interesting that you can share it with the whole class, hmmmm?" When this works (Ellen has used it successfully with gossiping police officers who were distracting the rest of the class), it makes everyone laugh, including the distracting talkers, and it also gets them to shut up and pay attention again. But it's tricky. If you're not overly-dramatic enough, the audience may not realize that you're kidding, and the distracting talkers may feel humiliated instead of gently teased.

Facilitators usually feel comfortable just moving toward the chattering pair; they may even come up behind them and obviously eavesdrop. If the pair are indeed talking about something related to the presentation, then the Facilitator can work their comments into the larger group. If they are chatting about the weather, or where one of them bought their new shoes, the Facilitator's mere physical presence will probably be enough to get them to desist the gabbing and get back with the program.

Professors can get the conversationalists back to attention easily by simply asking them a question. Now be careful here, Professors. It's not a good idea to ask unsuspecting members of your audience "test" questions. Suppose I truly haven't been paying attention to your talk on "Internet Marketing Opportunities for Small Businesses," so you decide to "punish" me by saying, "You there, next to the other person who is not paying attention: What percentage of increased sales can a small business expect from Internet marketing in the first year of web site develop-ment?" I'm probably going to have to say, in a small voice, "I don't know," and feel embarrassed and stupid. It's fine to have a Professor's style in certain circumstances, but it's never fine to treat audience members as though they were students trying to get a good grade.

So what question should you ask? An emotional question works best under these circumstances. (See Chapter 6.) Try this: "Excuse me, but I was just wondering, what might your particular concerns be about the future of Internet marketing?" This gives anyone who hasn't been pay-ing attention the chance to respond without fear of being "graded" on the answer.

We have an even better technique for you to use, one that will work well for all five styles, but especially for Orators and Preachers.

> ### Quick Tip:
> You can make people want to pay attention to you, by just involving them personally in your presentation. All you have to do is create a hypothetical example just for them.

It works like this: Suppose you are presenting an orientation for new hires and your part of the presentation is "The Corporate Health Plan and What It Means to You." And during your presentation, Bob and Carla start a side conversation that gradually begins to interfere with your concentration and your audience's. So you have to do something about it, and you decide to say, "Let's think about how this benefit I've been describing to you would work in real life. Suppose Bob and Carla here, for example, are a married couple. [Bob and Carla hear their names and immediately know that you are speaking about them.] And suppose Carla's elderly mother lives with them. Now let me explain just how this health plan benefit would help Bob and Carla pay for her mother's expensive medical treatments," and so on. Involve distracting audience members in a hypothetical situation and you'll have their attention for the rest of your talk. Guaranteed.

3. A member of the audience falls asleep during the most important part of the presentation.

Is the sleeper in the back row, not bothering anyone? Then let him or her sleep—what the heck. Maybe they had a bad night. Maybe they're not feeling well. Who cares, as long as they're not disturbing anyone.

Ah, but what if the sleeper is in the front of the room, where everyone can see him or her? And what if they're not just sleeping, but loudly snoring? Entertainers can't stand this kind of reaction—they always take it personally. (For them, it's like the story of the young playwright who invited a noted drama critic to the opening of his play. The critic came to opening night, but he slept through the entire performance. When the play was over, the young playwright angrily accosted the critic in the lobby of the theater. "How could you sleep through my play," whined the playwright, "when you know how much I value your opinion?" "My dear young man," replied the critic. "Sleep is an opinion!")

So what should an Entertainer do in this situation? Wake the person up and say something inane like, "You were so excited about coming to my session that you couldn't sleep last night, right?"

No, no, no. Falling asleep is the same as not paying attention. Thus, the best way to deal with this is to do exactly what you did for the people whispering to each other: Involve the inattentive ones in a hypothetical situation. The real key is just to call the person by name; wakes them right up and keeps them awake for awhile. Works every time, for every style.

4. An audience member's beeper goes off, or their cell phone rings.

Hard to believe that people could be so discourteous in this day and age, but there you are. Ellen once had a participant whose phone not only rang, but he picked it up and proceeded to carry on a conversation right in the middle of the session, right in the middle of the room, where everyone could see and hear (and be completely distracted).

This one's a little harder to just ignore, since the sound is always so startling. We're thinking that all five styles should try to adopt a little of the Entertainer's style for this one and come up with a cute, quick remark, and then let it drop. Here are a few comments to consider:

"If that's for me, tell them I'm not here."

"Tell them I want mine with mushrooms and extra cheese."

If you feel brave enough, you could also pretend to pick up your own phone and carry on a conversation with the person on the real phone: "So nice of you to call. Well, you see I'm in the middle of a presentation right now, so I can't really talk."

5. No one asks any questions during the Q&A period.

We've already covered this situation to some extent in Chapter 3. You'll remember (we hope!) that we basically offered you 2 options:

    a. Ask yourself a question to get them started.

    b. Go right to your conclusion.

Facilitators can avoid this whole problem by using a number of participatory techniques. Here are a few examples:

    a. Put people into groups (if they aren't there already) and ask the group to come up with a question. Then answer the question from each group.

    b. Ask participants to write a question on an index card. Then ask them to pile their cards on the table and mix them up. Then have one person draw one card and read the question aloud. You answer *that* question.

    c. Ask participants to write questions—as they think of them— on sticky notes and attach them to a flip chart or a wall at any time throughout the session (or at breaks, if you prefer). When it's time for the Q&A, just pick notes off the "Parking Lot" (as it is sometimes called.)

The possibilities are endless for Facilitators. For the other 4 styles, there is danger in "dead air." Entertainers, Professors, Orators, and Preachers will be tempted to "fill up the air" by rambling on or off on a tangent. RESIST THIS URGE! Just because they don't have any questions, you shouldn't feel compelled to make up answers. Go right to your conclusion.

6. An audience member asks you a question you can't answer.

We don't care how much of an Entertainer you are—don't try to bluff your way out of this one. And you Professor styles—don't try to befog your listeners with a seemingly related but not quite accurate response. (Both Entertainers and Professors loathe being wrong.) Orators may try to distract the questioner by the power of their prose, Preachers by the strength of their sincerity.

Usually Facilitators do the best with this problem; they merely seek out someone else in the audience who might know the answer, or else they simply say they don't know, but will try to find out and get back to the questioner. The other four styles should adopt this strategy. Simply say, "That's an excellent question. Wish I had an excellent answer."

7. An audience member asks a long, extremely complicated question or a series of questions.

Whew! These are tricky to deal with for any style. But they are particularly dangerous for Entertainers, who dread any sort of "dead air" while they're on stage, and are most likely to stop listening to the question halfway through and start rehearsing their answer. When the questioner is finally finished, the Entertainer will jump in with a rehearsed answer—sometimes an answer that has nothing to do with the actual question. Professors, Orators, and Preachers are also prone to this malady. "The opposite of talking isn't listening," the humorist Fran Leibowitz reminds us, "the opposite of talking is waiting." Waiting for your turn to talk, rehearsing your answer.

All four styles should take their cues from Facilitators here: If you've got a flip chart or a blank transparency or a white board handy, paraphrase the question in writing, with the help of the questioner. This will then allow you to address the question point by point, completely. Even if you don't have an a-v handy, just simply paraphrasing the question (or questions) before you begin to answer will have two beneficial results: First, a paraphrase will help you figure out exactly what it is the questioner wants to know. Second, a paraphrase will help you buy time while you figure out what the answer is.

8. Someone in your audience disagrees with you—and says so, loudly.

This is the closest most presenters get to a heckler situation. Once in a blue moon (it doesn't happen too often, thank goodness) an audience member will decide that he or she knows more than you, and instead of just leaving, will decide to prove it to the rest of the audience. Who knows why some people act this way (we suspect a troubled childhood), but you have to be prepared that it might happen to you.

As we mentioned earlier, you must consciously resist the urge to fire back at these rude people. What worked for Don Rickles on The Tonight Show will be certain death for you on the podium. Remember that you want to avoid alienating the audience at all costs. On the other hand, you will also have to come up with some sort of response for someone who is publically giving you a hard time.

> *Quick Tip:*
> If someone in the audience says, "Have you read the latest studies on that topic?" (asking you a test question), or "I don't think that any right-minded people in this nation would agree with your point of view," or "Where do people like you get off saying that about people like me?" or some such threat-disguised-as-a-question, you just do this: To yourself, inside your own mind, where no one can hear you but you, you say to yourself, "What would the question or comment really be if the person asking the question/making the comment were a decent human being?"

Now, this technique accomplishes two things: 1. It calms you down, lets you make (unseen and silent) fun of the heckler, and prevents you from coming right back with some stupid retort such as "Oh, yeah? Well, I suppose YOU know EVERYTHING." 2. It allows you to figure out a way to answer the question and get back to your objective, without being sidetracked by a jerk.

So, for example, suppose you do get the question, "How dare you people come in to our community and presume to lecture us about what is good for us?"

a. Take a deep breath, think, "What would the question be if the questioner were a decent human being?"
b. Decide that the "real" question is, "Will this new program take away some of our basic self-governing rights?"
c. Ask the questioner, "It sounds to me that you are worried that this new program will take away some of your historic

rights, is that correct? Well, let me assure you that....." and proceed to answer the "real" question. This technique works for all five styles.

9. They get distracted and stop paying attention to you.

Well, if you're an Entertainer, your first response will probably be similar to our Uncle Joe's. Uncle Joe was an incorrigible joke teller, and some of his close relatives (most notably his sister-in-law, our mother, Pat) were often subjected to hearing the same joke told for the umpteenth time. After awhile they would stop paying attention as soon as Uncle Joe would begin a joke for some new unsuspecting visitors. But Uncle Joe (a supreme Entertainer) couldn't bear to lose any member of his audience, and he would always stop the joke and yell, "Patsy! Patsy! Are you looking at me? Is everybody looking at me?!" Our Uncle Joe was a dear, but he was also a comic slave driver.

No, you can't yell at your audience to get their attention (although you can try raising your volume to bring them back). What you can try are some of these tricks:

a. Use a noise maker of some sort, such as a slide whistle, a bell, or a buzzer. Or turn the lights on and off. If you've done your homework and you anticipate that your audience is going to get rowdy, you can set up a signal with them ahead of time.

b. Just stop and be silent. Wait for them to notice that you're not saying anything. (Warning: This technique will either work brilliantly, or they'll continue ignoring you until the end of time. They won't even notice when you leave.)

c. Try Bob Pike's "hypnotic command" technique. To get an audience's attention back from a particularly rowdy participatory activity, Bob merely says, in a very soft voice, "When you hear the sound of my voice, please bring your attention back to the front of the room." As he repeats this over and over, little by little a few audience members at a time hear him and stop talking. It's sort of a sonic wave effect.

A final note: If you've established a good rapport with your audience from the beginning, you should be able to get them back on track fairly easily. After all, you're all in it together.

10. You realize that they are the wrong audience for your presentation.

This actually happened to one of our clients: He had been told by his boss to prepare a 30-minute presentation and tour of the factory for a group of visitors. He assumed the visitors would be representatives of his organization's client companies. They turned out to be a group of 5th-graders from a local school. Ooops.

Yes, yes, we know, and we know that you know that he should have done his homework, that he should not have assumed anything, that he should have asked more questions of his boss before preparing his presentation. Be that as it may, what was he supposed to do when he found out that he was completely unprepared for his particular audience? What would you do?

Improvise! Take the same material and make it meaningful to a bunch of teenagers! Entertainers and Professors can do this easily, if they're really attuned to their audience. Facilitators will get the audience talking right away, and so be able to turn the presentation into a discussion. Orators and Preachers will have a bit more difficult time of it, accustomed as they are to working from a more rigidly prepared script. Anyone can turn a potential speaking nightmare like this into a successful presentation if they're ready to TRANSLATE!

Want to see how easy this is? Get ready to play

The Translation Game

Directions: Below are 3 nonsense topics for speeches. Under each topic are listed 5 completely different audiences. By yourself (or better yet, with a group), start speaking on the first topic to the first audience. Speak for about a minute or so, then (still speaking on the same topic) instantly tailor your presentation to be meaningful to the next audience on the list, and so on.

Topic 1: Why seaweed is impractical for stuffing upholstery.

A. Dentists

B. Flight attendants

C. Computer analysts

D. Economists

E. Shoe salespeople

Topic 2: The influence of baroque architecture on Papago Indian dwellings.

A. Hot air balloon pilots

B. Elementary school teachers

C. Music video directors

D. Accountants

E. Pro golfers

Topic 3: The mating habits of the amoeba

A. Nuclear physicists

B. Newspaper editors

C. Webmasters

D. Cab drivers

E. Corporate CEOs

See how easy it is to shift from group to group? All you need to do is really *see* them in your mind, put yourself in their shoes, and imagine what might be important to them. Then just speak about that.

[Note: If you're doing this as a group exercise, debrief the exercise afterwards to determine any differences you noticed among the five presentation styles.]

Adapt Different Styles for Different Presentations

One size does not necessarily fit all when it comes to making superior presentations. What might work fabulously at an after-dinner talk, for example, might bomb disastrously at a mid-morning executive briefing. Just because you wowed 'em during your keynote speech at the conference doesn't guarantee that you will be equally successful with the same material and style at a public hearing.

Let's look at the somewhat unique presentation needs of a variety of speaking situations:

Sales Presentations
Briefings
Conference Sessions
Keynote Speeches
After-dinner talks
Public Hearings
Instructional Sessions

First, we'll sketch out the most common characteristics of these kinds of presentations, including the typical audience members for each (who), the usual objective (what), the logistics of the space (where), and the constraints of time (when). Then we'll consider which of the five presenter styles (or which combination of styles) will work most comfortably and effectively for each kind of presentation. Lastly, we'll list 5 Quick Tips for making each kind of presentation successful.

Sales Presentations with Style

Who

Obviously, potential customers will be your usual attendees. Although you may be dismayed to learn that no one in your audience has actual purchasing approval power, nevertheless those who are present may indeed be able to influence the absent decision-maker. If they "buy" your pitch, the decision-maker may actually buy your product. So it's worth the effort to pitch as persuasively as you can.

It goes without saying (although we're going to say it anyway) that you'll need to tailor your sales presentation to fit the expertise level of your audience. If you are trying, for example, to convince your audience of the impressive benefits of the Wham II system, you'll need to know how systems-literate they are. If they are "techies," they'll expect technical details, lots of data perhaps, loads of graphs and figures (and be prepared for lots of questions regarding your product's technical capabilities). If they are mechanically-declined types (users rather than technical experts), they may need more pictorials, analogies, or anecdotes. They will probably also ask fewer technical questions.

If, as is most likely, your sales presentation audience will be "mixed"—experts and newbies, techies and users—you have a bit more of a problem. All things not being equal, given an audience with varying levels of expertise, whom do you talk to?

You talk to the decision-makers, of course, if any are present. (You will, of course, have done your homework here. You will know in advance who the decision-makers are and whether or not they will attend. If you haven't determined this beforehand, you'd better do it in the first two minutes of your presentation.)

What

The objective for any sales presentation is the same: "Buy my product—tangible or intangible, thing or idea." A sales presentation is out-and-out a persuasive presentation, and its design follows a justification structure (with lots of reasons why).

Here's what the Presentation Diamond™ looks like for a sales presentation:

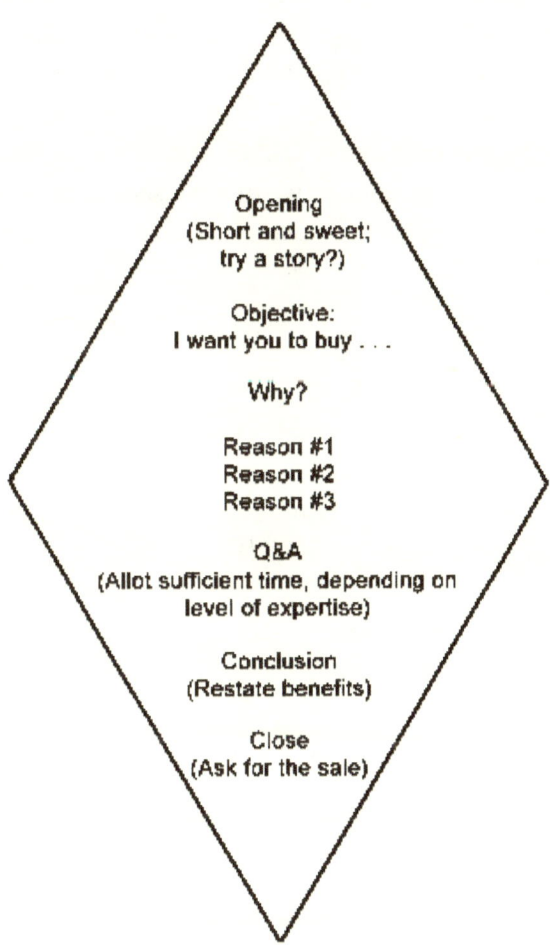

Opening
(Short and sweet;
try a story?)

Objective:
I want you to buy . . .

Why?

Reason #1
Reason #2
Reason #3

Q&A
(Allot sufficient time, depending on
level of expertise)

Conclusion
(Restate benefits)

Close
(Ask for the sale)

Where

Sales presentations usually take place in a conference room or meeting room, sometimes in the clients' offices, sometimes in yours. If you have a choice, do all you can to avoid making a sales presentation in any one person's office. You don't want to be presenting in any particular person's "territory."

For a successful sales presentation, it is imperative that you be able to set up the space before your audience arrives. (See Chapter 4.) You want to be able to make the space your own, and to then welcome your audience as their host. You want to be able to arrange the furniture so that everyone can see and hear you comfortably. Most importantly, you want to be able to test your audio visuals and make sure that everything is working perfectly. Any glitch in your presentation, however small, may suggest to your potential customers that your product may be equally flawed.

If, by some sad chance, you are not able to set up the space before your audience arrives, then just keep it very simple. No complicated audio visuals, no tricky gadgets, no high-production values. Don't include anything that could possibly break down, and you'll feel a lot more comfortable and appear much more confident. (This won't work, of course, if your product is a complicated, tricky gadget! Then all we can say is that it better work perfectly!)

When

Most sales presentations take place during normal business hours. Thus, most attendees will be in their normal-business-hours-working-mode and relatively inclined to listen to your pitch (as opposed to potential customers who are at home, in their jammies, eating dinner, and not at all inclined to listen to a disruptive telemarketer's pitch).

If you have any control over the time of day scheduled for your presentation, choose early to mid-morning, when most people's energy levels are at their highest. Avoid, if you can, the "after lunch slump," or the "I'm-hungry-when-can-we-break-for-lunch" spot. Late afternoon may be good or bad, depending. Sometimes people are tired and just want to go home, so they could either turn you down to get rid of you, or buy your product to get rid of you—it could go either way. (The presenter with style, of course, does a little investigation before the presentation to learn what time of the day the decision-maker normally makes decisions.)

Presentation Style

Depending on the audience, a combination of styles will work most effectively for sales presentations. But you should consider adding a significant amount of Entertainer to the mix. Most people are not aware that storytelling can be a powerful persuasive technique for selling. If you feel it's appropriate to get an emotional response from your audience, then tell them a story that will convince them to buy your product or idea.

For example, back in 1987, the Manager of Sales and Management Training for Porsche Cars of North America compiled a collection of stories called "Porsche Anecdotes," to be used as a resource for the marketing and advertizing staff. The salespeople at Porsche use these stories to build value for their cars.

Does every product or service have a story? Absolutely! And selling, at its most basic level, is telling that story—appealing to the potential buyer's emotional as well as informational needs.

Usually a Facilitator style won't be too effective for a sales presentation. Your audience doesn't want to listen to each other—they want to hear what you have to say. A notable exception to this advice will occur if, for some strange reason, you suddenly realize that no one in your audience is a decision-maker and that none of them have any interest at all in your product. Or maybe they don't even know that your product exists (it's so new) and so have no idea whether they need it or not. If this worst-case scenario occurs, you might get much better results by switching roles immediately from Sales Presenter to Focus Group Facilitator. Put your audience into groups, ask them to brainstorm their needs and concerns, tell them you'll collect their responses, and then schedule another time to come back and make a sales presentation to a (by then) informed audience.

These minor modifications aside, a good sales presenter is a combination of Preacher and Professor. You've got to be an evangelist for your product; you've got to want to convince your audience that they can be "saved" (from drudgery, from loss of revenue, from inferior manufacturing, etc.) by the grace of your product. Concurrently, you want to present the benefits of your product or proposal in a systematic, thoroughly researched, eminently professorial way. You want to lay it out logically for them, and you want to convince them to convert.

> ## 5 Quick Tips for Sales Presentations with Style:
>
> 1. Get to the point quickly. After an extremely short opening (maybe as simple as "Good morning"), state your objective. Don't play games with your audience; they know why you're there.
> 2. Try to schedule your presentation for early or mid-morning. Decision-makers are more likely to make decisions during these times.
> 3. Set up the space in advance so that you and your audience both feel comfortable.
> 4. Rehearse with your equipment. If something goes wrong with one of your audio-visual aids, be prepared to just ignore the problem and continue without it. Don't make jokes; don't apologize; don't make a federal case. Just get on with it.
> 5. Tell your audience exactly how long your presentation is going to last, and then stick to the schedule. You are allowed to vary from this rule only if the decision-maker specifically asks you to continue past your stated closing time.

Briefings with Style

Who

People attend briefings when they need information or want an update. Audiences can include military or law enforcement personnel preparing for a mission; executives preparing for a new company strategy; or middle managers preparing for a new round of company layoffs.

Typically, people attending a briefing will be there of their own volition: They want to know what's going on, what's new, what's up, or what the plan is. Typically, they will be interested in the topic and anxious to learn something they don't already know.

Nevertheless, briefings can be deadly if they are not tailored for their specific audiences. For example, your briefing to internal managers on next year's planned upgrades for the Wham II will need to be designed with your specific audience's level of expertise in mind. Will they be able to understand high-tech jargon? Or will you have to speak to them as though they were "normal human beings." When you work through your "Mind Rehearsal" for this kind of presentation, remember to pay particular attention to the question, "What will they want to learn?" Your answer to this question will determine significantly how you should customize your briefing for this particular audience.

What

In our definition, briefings (unlike sales presentations) are informative presentations. They may also be somewhat instructional, since one major goal of teaching is the passing on of information. However, we will distinguish here between an informative objective and an instructional one (which we will cover in detail in the section on Instructional Sessions in this chapter).

An informative presentation uses a "main point" internal structure. Present two or three significant aspects of your topic and then open the discussion up for Q&A. (Oh, and did we mention this? By their very nature, BRIEFINGS SHOULD BE BRIEF.)

Here's what the Presentation Diamond™ looks like for a briefing:

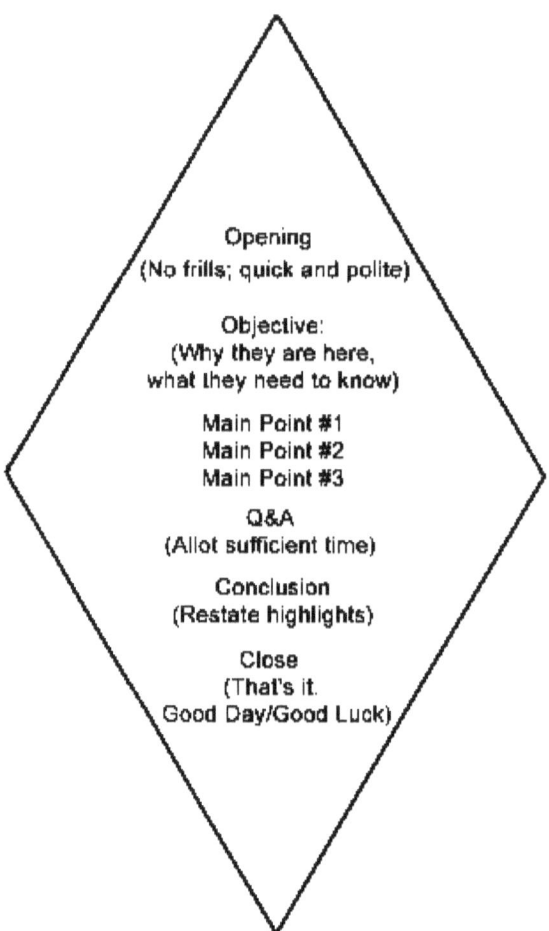

Opening
(No frills; quick and polite)

Objective:
(Why they are here,
what they need to know)

Main Point #1
Main Point #2
Main Point #3

Q&A
(Allot sufficient time)

Conclusion
(Restate highlights)

Close
(That's it.
Good Day/Good Luck)

Where

Typically, briefings, like sales presentations, take place in conference rooms (in some cases actually called "briefing rooms") and the like. As with sales presentations, try to avoid holding a briefing in any one person's territory—a neutral space will help keep things objective.

Conducting your briefing in a neutral space will also make it easier for you to set the stage before your audience arrives. Many briefings include examples and illustrations (maps, flight plans, protocols, etc.), and you need to make sure ahead of time that your foils are easy to see from anywhere in the room, that your LCD is functioning properly, and that your charts and graphs are clear and readable.

When

Briefings typically take place during normal business hours, as with sales presentations. However, briefings can sometimes be scheduled close on the heels of an unplanned event. If your company experiences an unexpected environmental problem, for example, you may find yourself conducing a briefing on "How We Plan to Deal with this Hazard" at any time of the day—or night. (We assume that if you are conducting a briefing on "How to Get Out of this Building Without Choking to Death on Toxic Fumes," your audience will be interested in what you have to say, whether you are speaking in the middle of the morning or the middle of the night.)

Presentation Style

The Professor style would, at first glance, seem ideal for briefings. Indeed, a briefing can be constructed like a mini-lecture (main points and illustrations). Your audience comes to you to learn something they don't already know, much as students come to class to learn the cause of the fall of the Roman Empire or the mating habits of the amoeba.

The main thing Professors have to watch out for when conducting a briefing is their timing. We are reminded of a cartoon we once saw where a Professor in robe and mortar board begins a speech by saying, "I know so much I don't know where to begin." Yes, you're the expert. Yes, you know more that they do, yes they are most likely to be interested in what you have to say. But if you drone on too long (we think over 15 minutes is too long for most briefings), you'll lose them. Resist the urge to tell them EVERYTHING. Do your homework and just tell them what they need to know.

What about the other styles? A little Entertainer at the opening or close might be good, as long as your topic is not too serious. ("A funny thing happened to me on the way to the nuclear meltdown . . ." is probably not a good way to start.) A little Entertainer during the data part of the briefing might also help keep their eyes from glazing over (especially if the topic of your briefing is "Update on How to Fill out the New Insurance Forms"). A little Preacher might likewise help if you need to "pump them up" for superior performance after the briefing. ("Now get out there and make those mousepads squeak!") Consider putting on your Facilitator hat during the Q&A, especially if some of your audience members are also experts who can answer questions that you can't. But leave your Orator style at home: Your audience has come to learn, not to be impressed by your vocal dexterity.

---

5 Quick Tips for Briefings with Style:

1. Live up to the title: Keep it BRIEF.
2. Spend as much time as you can researching what your audience already knows about your topic.
3. Translate technical terms for non-technical audiences.
4. Illustrate to illuminate, not just to dump data on your audience.
5. Make sure that all of your audio visuals can be read easily by all of your audience. And keep them as simple as possible, with a little humor (if appropriate).

Conference Presentations with Style

Who

As with briefings, conferences are attended by people who want to gather information, learn something new, or get an update on things already familiar to them. So they will be expecting some lecture, some demonstration, and some evidential data to support your presentation's objectives.

A particular kind of conference presentation is the academic research presentation, where colleagues from various disciplines gather to share their discoveries, glean new information for their own research, and check out what their peers have been up to.

But conference attendees usually expect more than just a series of sessions: They also expect opportunities to network with their co-attendees. Indeed, Harrison Owen thinks that this aspect of a conference—the networking and sharing of information that occurs between attendees between sessions—is so vital to a conference's success that he devised a meeting technology known as the "Open Space Conference." (See Chapter 10.)

As Owen sees it, all conferences (including academic conferences) are governed by "The Law of Two Feet"—attendees are free to treat the conference as their own personal education smorgasbord: a little of this, a little of that, two minutes at this session (it's boring), an hour at that (it's more interesting). Many attendees prefer to sit in the back of the room for this very reason. They give the speaker a few minutes to demonstrate whether or not the session will be of interest to them, and then if they decide it won't, they're out the door, looking for another session. The audience at a conference presentation brings with it a certain mobility not ordinarily found at other types of presentations.

Additionally, it's much harder to anticipate your audience's needs at a conference, since the people who attend your session may come from very varied backgrounds. Some may be newbies to the field, looking for basic information. Others may be oldtimers, looking to sharpen the skills they already possess. The rest will display a wide variety of interests, skills, and levels of expertise. Therefore, it's imperative that you do some surveying in the first moments of your presentation to see what exactly you have in your room at the moment.

Mike recently sat in on a conference on "The Internet," accompanied by other academics, researchers, industry people, and government officials. A top executive from a very famous computer software giant that shall remain nameless, who was supposed to be talking about "The Future of the Internet" instead spent 30 minutes explaining what the Internet is and its history, as if his audience were a group of grade school students or recent immigrants from central Asia or something. We don't care how big your company is. Do your homework.

What

Because conference attendees may have been "born to wander," presenters need to structure their talks to accomplish two important objectives:

1. Make people want to stay through the entire session. (A little Entertainer, a little Preacher will help.)
2. And if they do stay, make sure they leave with useful information that they can take back to work. (Mike likes to remind his business students, "PowerPoint and animation effects are great for entertainment value, but will not make up for a lack of content.")

Here is how the Presentation Diamond™ looks for a conference presentation:

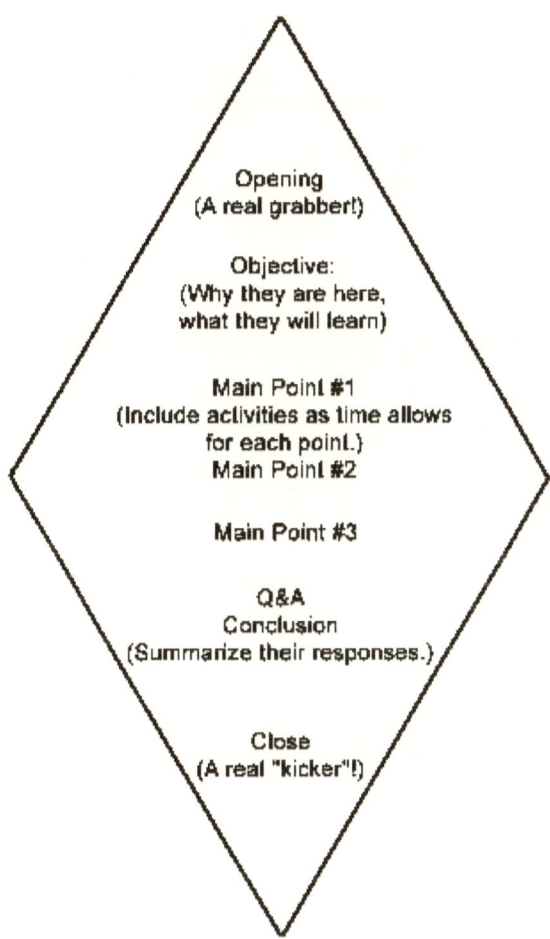

Opening
(A real grabber!)

Objective:
(Why they are here,
what they will learn)

Main Point #1
(Include activities as time allows
for each point.)
Main Point #2

Main Point #3

Q&A
Conclusion
(Summarize their responses.)

Close
(A real "kicker"!)

Where

Logistics can be a nightmare for conference presenters, particularly since you'll have little control over any aspect—where you present, when you present, how big the room is, how the chairs are set up, and so forth, will all be determined well before you arrive. Here's a partial list of the headaches you may encounter:

1. The room will be huge, seating up to 500 people, and only 20 people will show up for your presentation. And they'll all sit in the back.
2. The room will be small, seating up to 50 people, and 500 people will show up for your session. And hold you personally responsible for the fact that there are no more chairs.
3. The room will be too hot or too cold.
4. In a big room, your microphone won't work at all.
5. In a small room, your microphone will be too loud.
6. Your room will be separated from the rooms on either side by walls made of Japanese rice paper. (And in one of the rooms right next to you they'll be showing a video. REALLY LOUD.)
7. People won't be able to find the room and will arrive late and will have to crawl over other people to reach the only seats left in the front row.
8. These same people will realize after five minutes that they don't want to be there and they'll have to crawl back over the same people to get out.

The only really good news here is that usually you will have some time—15 minutes to a half-hour between sessions—so that you can get into the space after the previous speaker finishes and set up the space for yourself before the majority of your audience arrives. During this setup time, you can follow the procedure we outlined for you in Chapter 4. (If you're speaking to 500 people and you're really nervous, just rearrange 500 chairs and you'll calm right down!)

And for heaven's sake, use this time to rehearse with your own technology! Mike has seen several presenters spend a long time trying to find out how to turn on the overhead projector. One guy finally got it on, Mike relates, but his transparency was upside down. He didn't notice it until someone from the audience pointed it out. This leads us to "Dowling's Law of the Overhead": Put your transparency on the overhead and then TURN AROUND AND LOOK AT IT. (We're ashamed that we even have to say this.)

When

The timing for a conference presentation is always predetermined, usually 1 to 1½ hours. If you run overtime on your session, you'll make your attendees late for their next session.

According to Mike (who teaches in German in Germany), the Germans have a saying: "A Professor can talk over anything, as long as it's not over 30 minutes." (*Ein deutscher Professor kann über alles reden, aber nich über 30 Minuten!* Mike says it's funnier in German.)

The time of day you are scheduled to speak will vary widely at a conference. You may be scheduled to present on the first day of a three-day conference, on the last day, or any day (or time) in between. You may find yourself presenting in the early morning (7 a.m.), late in the afternoon, or on a Saturday or Sunday. It just depends on what choices the conference designers have made. Usually they will not have asked you for your preference.

There are advantages and disadvantages to presenting at a conference at different times. Let's examine some of these:

Time of Day/Day of Week	Advantage	Disadvantage
Early morning	People may be more energetic and alert because it's early.	People may be groggy and slow because it's early and they stayed up too late last night socializing with their co-attendees.
Late morning	People may be right in the middle of their most energetic period of the day.	People may be distracted by their growling stomachs because they haven't had lunch yet.
Early afternoon	People may be re-invigorated by their lunch break and ready to learn again.	People may be complacently sated by their lunch and ready to nap.
Late afternoon	People may be comfortable with the conference format by now and ready to learn in high gear.	People may be burned out by now and ready to head to the bar for happy hour.
First day of the conference	People are eager to get the most out of their attendance, and they are energetic and attentive.	People are anxious that they'll not be able to get into certain popular sessions, and they are cranky and hostile.
Last day of the conference	People are seasoned learners by now and they are truly motivated to get the most out of your session.	People are at the bar, the amusement park, or on their way home, having burned out completely.

So you see, it's a toss-up. You just need to do the best you can with the time and place assigned to you.

Presentation Style

Of all the different kinds of presentations, a conference session has the most unknowns. You may not know for sure who will attend your session; you may not have any choice about the day or time of your presentation; and you probably will have little or no say about the room setup. With all these variables, it's important to have all five of the Presentation Styles at your beck and call, ready to be summoned to help you deal with whatever you encounter.

The Professor style is needed to get your points across and to illustrate them with convincing evidence. But too much Professor can be deadly at those times of the day when your attendees may be most distracted by outside temptations.

A bit of the Entertainer is invaluable for convincing people to stay for awhile and for livening up any otherwise doze-inducing data dumps. But too much Entertainer can leave your audience feeling that they got a lot of dessert but no entree. They want to learn something, not just be amused.

Orator style works nicely for openings and closings, especially with large groups. Particularly important is the Orator's closing, because you want your audience to leave your session remembering your "famous last words." Orator style should be used sparingly, however. Remember that your audience wants to take away a concept or two, not simply be taken away by the force of your verbiage.

A little Preacher is good, in small doses, for those "downtime" sections of the day, when you need a little passion to "pump them up." Nothing convinces as much as conviction, and Preachers have conviction to spare. Too much sales pitching can get tiring, however, particulary for those audiences who have been pitched at for lo these many hours and are simply conferenced-out.

We've saved Facilitator for last because it is not used nearly as much as it should be at conferences. Remember the "Open Space" concept we talked about earlier and the fact that the conference attendees frequently learn more from each other than from any of the conference speakers? This is why it's such a good idea to give them opportunities to do the same thing in your session. Any activity, no matter how short or informal ("Now, let's get in small groups and discuss…") can be a terrific learning experience for your audience. Plus, facilitated exercises during your session have the same effect as the Entertainer's storytelling, the Preacher's passion, or the Orator's poetry: They energize the audience so that they will be alert and receptive to learning. (For other resources on how to design and deliver a participatory conference session, see Chapter 10.)

> ### 5 Quick Tips for Conference Presentations with Style:
>
> 1. Always get to your room as early as you can to set up and "take the space."
> 2. Try to be more of a Facilitator than a Professor, particularly at the low-energy-level times of the day.
> 3. Don't be bothered by people who sit in the back and leave early. Just consider them "tourists."
> 4. Ask any early arrivals to your session to help you check your audio visuals' readability and your microphone levels.
> 5. Delight them with your style, but make sure you teach them something, too!

Keynote Speeches with Style

Who

Since a keynote speech is usually used to kick off or conclude a conference of some sort, the folks who attend have probably come together because of some common interest or because they are in the same career field. So you might find yourself delivering the opening keynote to the assembled members of the American Society for Training and Development at its annual International Conference and Exposition. Or you might be asked to deliver the concluding keynote to participants who have registered for a week-long conference on governmental regulations and their impact on individual communities. In this respect, keynote speeches are very similar to conference presentations, in that the audience will be relatively homogenous (all members of the same professional society) as well as relatively heterogenous (each having different needs, concerns, and levels of expertise). You'll just have a lot more of them: While 50 people may show up for your conference session, 500 may be there for your keynote (or 5000, depending on the size of the conference).

What

The major difference between a keynote speech at a conference and one of the actual conference presentations lies in their differing objectives. Your objective for a conference presentation, you will remember, is two-fold: 1. Make people want to stay through the entire session; and 2. Make sure they learn something useful they can take back to work. The objective for a keynote speech is, essentially, much more encompassing.

The very word, keynote, indicates that you'll be dealing with the BIG ISSUES in this presentation. The term comes from music, where the "keynote" is the first note of every scale, the note that gives the scale its name and lets us refer to certain pieces of music as composed in the key of C or D or E or etc. It is thus the most important note, the "key" to the whole piece. The term has also come to mean "a prime underlying element or theme" and has eventually evolved into "keynote address," which is "an opening address, as at a political convention, that outlines the issues to be considered" (*American Heritage Dictionary*). The keynote address can either kick off the whole conference by giving attendees an overview of what to expect, or it can conclude the whole conference by reminding attendees of what they've learned.

You want to accomplish at least three objectives with a keynote speech:

1. Pump them up and get them excited about the actual conference to come.
2. Remind them of why they came in the first place.
3. Assure them that their investment of time, energy, and money to participate will return to them a thousandfold.

Here's what the Presentation Diamond™ looks like for a keynote address:

Introduction

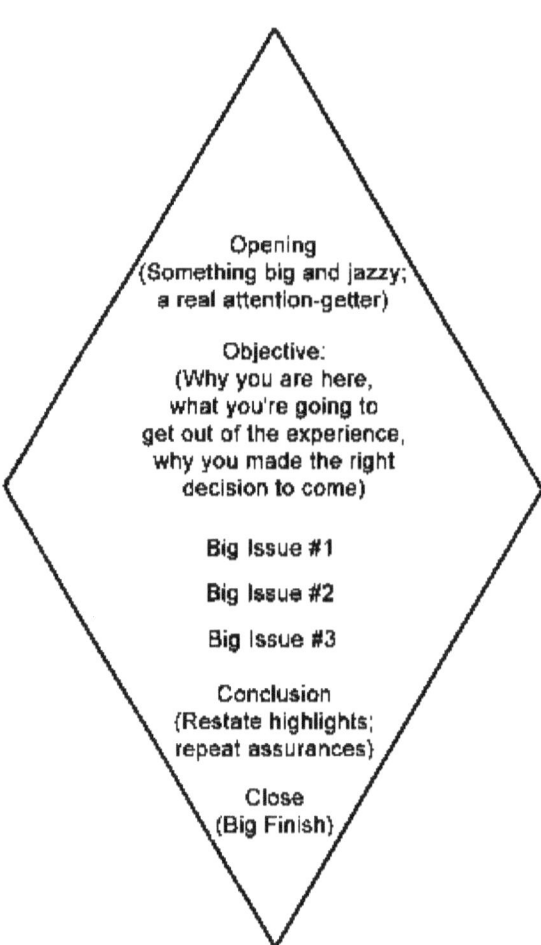

Opening
(Something big and jazzy;
a real attention-getter)

Objective:
(Why you are here,
what you're going to
get out of the experience,
why you made the right
decision to come)

Big Issue #1

Big Issue #2

Big Issue #3

Conclusion
(Restate highlights;
repeat assurances)

Close
(Big Finish)

You'll notice that we've added an "Introduction" section to the top of this Diamond. This is the part of your presentation that you don't personally deliver—someone else usually introduces you. We have one major piece of advice for you concerning introductions: WRITE YOUR OWN. Why take a chance that the person introducing you, no matter how well intentioned, might start everything off on the wrong foot? "Dear Abby" once reported a case where a well-meaning introducer began with, "Well, we had hoped to have [Dr. Really Famous] come to speak to us today, but he couldn't make it, so we have [Dr. Second Best] instead." How would you like to be that speaker? Or what if the introducer has some not-so hidden grudge against you and introduces you by saying, "What can be said about our next speaker that hasn't been said behind her back already?" You see our point?

Write your own introduction. Include information that will be interesting and relevant to your audience, and that will establish your credibility. Don't include any humor or stories; you can add them yourself when you begin speaking. And because you have to presume that your introducer will actually *read* your introduction, keep it short (half a page) and type it up in really big type so that even the most myopic of introducers can read it easily. (It would also be a good idea to spell out phonetically any unfamiliar words or terms.)

Once you have been successfully introduced, the rest is up to you, and you need to pay attention to how long you have to speak. The timing for a keynote speech is always predetermined, usually around 30 minutes or so, about the same as a briefing. Indeed, you can think of a keynote as a sort of "briefing with pyrotechnics"—your objective is to give attendees an overview of what they'll be getting out of the rest of the conference, but you also want to make them glad they came and get them enthused about participating. You can't really accomplish either of these goals if you drone on, professor-like, for hours. Stick to short and dynamic.

Thus, your opening and close need to be whizz-bang effective. This is probably why so many keynoters think it's a good idea to start with a joke; if the joke works, you've got them laughing, you've got them interested, and you've got them enthused. Mission accomplished.

But remember what we said about jokes way back in Chapter 2? If your joke flops in a room with 20 participants, imagine what it would be like in a room with 500 scowling people. You know what to do: Start with a great story, one that will immediately engage your audience and allow you to demonstrate your Entertainer style. Then, if you can use the story again in your close, you will have delivered a decisive keynote knockout punch. You can also start with a fabulous audio visual, but remember that a story is always going to be a lot less risky, especially in front of 5,000 people.

Here's a cool tip for organizing your "Big Issue" points in a keynote presentation: Hang them on an acronym. Suppose, for example, you have been asked to deliver the keynote address to the International Association of Team Leaders, a professional society composed of people who organize other people into teams. This is their annual conference, and they've just gone through a reorganization of their society's structure. Not everyone is comfortable with the new structure, and they're a little edgy about how well the conference will turn out, what with people's concerns and skepticisms. So you decide to organize your keynote around the very word TEAM.

You start by telling a grabber of a story about some team that was having problems but persevered and made it, and then you discuss your objective, which is to help them understand what TEAM really means. Then you associate a key concept with each of the letters in the word TEAM. Like this, for example:

T=Time. (It takes a great time commitment; it takes a long time before you see results.)

E=Energy (It takes extraordinary energy on the part of team members to keep the team going.)

A=Action (Nothing can be done if everyone just sits around talking about what to do.)

M=Motivation (Ya gotta wanna make the team succeed.)

And for each of these letters and concepts, you also attach a little story, or anecdote, or visual illustration, some of which can be humorous, some dramatic. Then, when it's time for your conclusion (it's quite rare to include a Q&A in a keynote speech), all you have to do is sum up your acronym and remind your audience of what the letters mean.

Cool, eh? This technique works like a charm everytime. It's especially good for speaking situations such as commencement addresses or any sort of "pump you up" presentation. (Ellen used this device very successfully in her kick-off presentation to 500 volunteers from the annual United Way campaign.)

Where

Since keynote addresses tend to be delivered to an assembled mass of attendees, they are usually conducted in large halls. The bigger the venue, the greater the risk of things going wrong. Hence, we think you ought to think twice about that fabulous high tech opening you were planning. Storytelling is your best bet, especially since you'll no doubt be wearing a microphone, and you can do really interesting things with your voice. (Make sure you get a lavalier microphone, so that you can get out from behind the podium!)

With a space so large, you might think that you would be strictly constrained to stand behind the podium. Not necessarily so—depending on the room set up, you may have lots of room to wander out into your audience. (Remember how successful one-time presidential candidate Elizabeth Dole was at doing just this?) Just make certain that they can see you; if you have to stay up on the "stage" to be seen, stay there. But don't block your body with a piece of furniture, if you can help it.

When

The kickoff keynote occurs at the beginning of the conference, and this opening time can vary widely. Sometimes you'll be speaking the evening before, and the conference will officially start (with concurrent sessions) the following morning. Or you'll be scheduled to speak in the morning, and the conference will start as soon as you've finished. In either case, the dynamics of the time of day are similar to those for any conference session: Early to mid-morning, attendees may be more wide awake and interested. Late afternoon to evening, they may be tired from traveling to get there, or distracted by the siren call of the hotel lobby bar.

[Horror story note: We once attended a conference where the kickoff keynote was scheduled for 7:00 in the evening, after most attendees had already traveled long distances that day just to get there, and after many of them had already spent two hours socializing in the lobby at an open bar. In other words, the majority of the audience was a bit tipsy and pretty tired. What did the keynote presenter do? She delivered a "state of the society" high Professor-style presentation, replete with boring overhead transparencies with boring bar graphs. LOTS of boring transparencies, with LOTS of boring bar graphs. Needless to say, those audience members who were tired began to drift off to sleep or to their rooms; those who were feeling antsy after a few drinks snuck back out to the bar. No energy, no enthusiasm, no style. The conference had not yet begun, and the attendees were ready to go home.]

When a keynote address concludes a presentation, your task is to get people excited about where they've been during the conference, what they've learned, and what they're planning to take back with them. Not many people will be with you for the finale—quite a few may have headed out early to the airport—but those who remain, by gosh, will be a dedicated audience. So your task is not that difficult. Just structure your remarks around the concept of "action plans." Ask them (rhetorically) what they're going to do with what they've learned, or (better yet) ask them to devise and/or sign a contract with themselves to keep their promises. Again, storytelling is your best bet to conclude a conference; it provides a little last bit of emotional oompahpah to help them "carry the torch forward" (so to speak). No lecturing, please. It's too late for that, anyway. Just give them some famous last words and be done with it.

Presentation Style

Forget your Professor mortar board when you accept an invitation to deliver a keynote address. The last thing anyone wants at the beginning or end of a conference is to be lectured to. By now you should agree that a major dollop of Entertainer will work best, with some sprinklings of Orator over a substantial helping of Preacher. After all, you want to convince them first, pump them up second, and leave them with words to live by last.

Most people would not consider facilitating a keynote address because they would assume that the size of the room and the large number of participants would be too logistically awkward. Not true! Even 500 people, if they are seated at round tables and can see each other easily, can be asked to "talk among yourselves" on one of your key points, and can then be debriefed by assistants who take a microphone from table to table. (You'll only have time for a few tables to report in, but you'll still be facilitating effectively.)

Maybe it's just trainers who are this crazy, but we've seen a closing keynote where the speaker encouraged her audience to participate in a series of zany exercises, to the extent that, at one point, people were actually standing up on their chairs and shouting. Talk about your high energy level! Perhaps attendees at the National Association of Federal Tax Auditors might not want to get this involved, but—hey—it's worth a shot.

> ### 5 Quick Tips for Keynotes Speeches with Style:
>
> 1. Avoid lecturing. Inspire and delight with stories and vivid illustrations.
> 2. If you're not already a member, make sure you learn all you can about the organization you'll be speaking to, particularly their concerns and dreams.
> 3. Keep it simple. Wow them with your personal style, not your audio visuals.
> 4. Consider devising interactive activities, even with very large groups.
> 5. Make them glad they came. Make them want to come back next year (or send others).

After-Dinner Talks with Style

Also known as "programs" or "meeting presentations" for professional society meetings, examples of this kind of presentation can also include "roasts" or "toasts"—celebrations of one person's life or achievements or whatnots. In our definition, this kind of presentation includes any speech (or "talk") given after people have eaten (or are still eating) breakfast, lunch, or dinner.

Who

Usually, audience members have been *invited* (not *told*) to attend. Thus, while the objective of your talk might be instructional ("The Seven Habits of Highly Destructive Teenagers," for example, to a group of parents), the participants have all come because they want to learn; no one has required them to do so or risk a poor performance review.

So attendees at these kinds of presentations can be quite delightful—already engaged and interested.

On the other hand, they can also be widely varied in their specific concerns and levels of expertise. "How to Install a SCSI Card in Three Easy Steps" might not work for a group that does not know what a SCSI card is; on the other hand, it might be just the thing for a group of people who are all about to buy scanners. As with any audience, homework is essential for this group.

Typically, you may not be a member of the group yourself. You may be the "Pro from Dover" who has been invited to speak to the group because of your fame in some area. In this case, it is even more important that you research your audience's concerns, general knowledge, and potential responses so that you can illustrate your talk with allusions and anecdotes that will be meaningful to them. Much like a standup comic, you will get good results if you tell them what they already know about themselves. (Review what we discussed about rapport in Chapter 6.)

What

[Note: You will probably be introduced before you speak. See our previous comments about writing your own introduction.]

The main objective of an after-dinner talk is to entertain and maybe throw in a little learning. Think of your talk as intellectual dessert—not too heavy, but not puff pastry, either. A nice cheesecake, maybe—substantial, but topped with a light cherry glaze.

Too many food metaphors, yes? Enough.

Let's get right to the Presentation Diamond™ for an After-Dinner Talk:

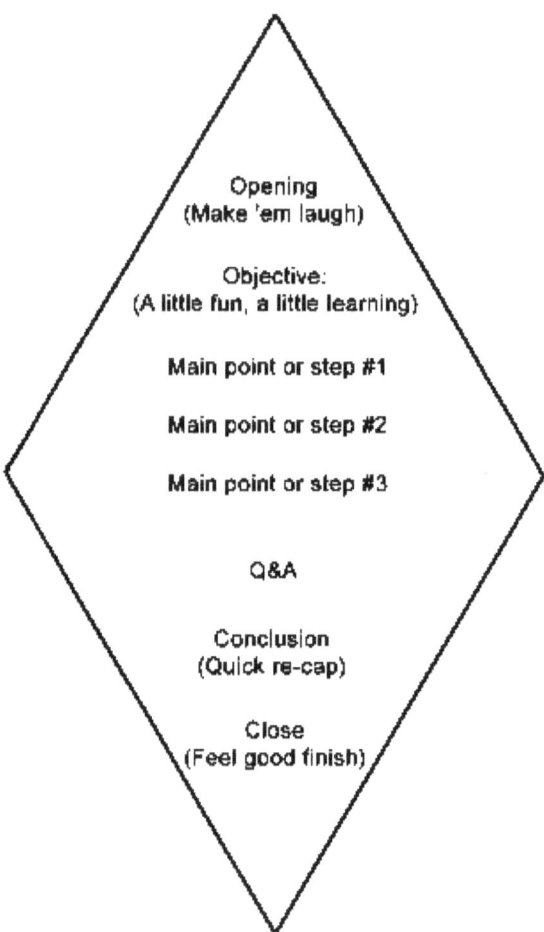

Opening
(Make 'em laugh)

Objective:
(A little fun, a little learning)

Main point or step #1

Main point or step #2

Main point or step #3

Q&A

Conclusion
(Quick re-cap)

Close
(Feel good finish)

Your opening and close should be as light-hearted as possible. Here's where your storytelling prowess will really pay off. You don't have much time, however (after-dinner talks should only be about 30-45 minutes, max), so don't launch into any really involved sagas. If possible, tell a personal story about yourself, as that will help you establish immediate rapport with the audience if you are unfamiliar to them personally. A related closing will increase your chances of getting a standing ovation!

Tell your audience right up front that your objective is not to overwhelm them with data or details, but simply to provide an overview, or a sample taste of something much bigger. And caution them that they might actually have fun!

If you are going to teach some sort of lesson during your program, make sure the protocol is as simple as possible. In fact, put the word "simple" or "easy" in the title of your talk: It will help reassure those audience members who don't feel technically up-to-snuff; it will intrigue those members who think they already know everything. ("Humph," they'll think. "How can anyone make that process SIMPLE?")

Go through your files and find all the humorous audio-visual illustrations you can. Insert them strategically throughout your presentation, to keep the momentum going and the pace hopping. And consider maybe at least one (short!) interactive activity. If you can pull this off, you'll keep even the most tired attendees awake and interested.

You may not get too many questions, depending on the time of day you are presenting. (If it's later in the evening, they may all just want to get it over with and go home.) On the other hand, you may get lots of response from a particularly engaged audience. Just watch your time and ask people to meet with you after the session for further discussions.

Where

These kinds of presentations, as we said above, always take place while people are eating. So usually you're in a meeting room or "banquet room" of some sort, with round tables covered with dishes and other assorted dining doo-dads. Although the tables may be large, they'll usually be so covered with foodstuff that there won't be much room left over for handouts or other materials. Plan your presentation accordingly.

If people are sitting at round tables, many of them may have their backs to you. Before you begin your official presentation, give them a few minutes to rearrange their chairs, so no one goes home complaining that the session "needed better ergonomic design." Make sure they're comfortable before you begin.

The biggest pain about these kinds of presentations is that, most likely, people will still be eating when you begin to speak. So you'll be competing with the cheesecake or the carrotcake. (Or the leftover chicken-ish entree.) And worst of all, you'll be competing with the servers who are bustling about, clanking cups and glasses, whispering "Do you want coffee?" and in general providing a major distraction. What to do?

IGNORE THEM. Your audience will be trying to pretend they are not there. You pretend, too. After all, it's not your fault that this hustle and bustle is going on; it's a necessary evil and everyone knows it. Don't try to embarrass the poor wait staff by commenting on their performance. Saying, "Oh, is the dishwasher leaving early tonight?" to one of the servers seems like a bad idea to us. Even worse: "I'd like to introduce my wife/husband. We have an agreement: I speak and he/she clears the table." Gag.

Just project your voice loudly enough to be heard clearly over any clatter and make yourself and your material so interesting that your audience won't want to look at or listen to anything else.

When

After breakfast. After lunch. After dinner. Which would you choose?

Lots of professional society meetings are now taking place at breakfast. Lots of business people like to get it over with so they can get back to their day. You can probably expect a high degree of interest and energy from most people at this time of the day, as well. (You just have to want to be "up" that early yourself.)

An after-lunch program is also good for audience energy, but time constraints get a little tighter here. People will expect the food, the meeting, and the program to be ON TIME, so that they won't be late getting back to work. Overall, however, this time of the day is usually a productive one, both for the audience and the speaker.

After-dinner is the most problematical, time-of-day-wise. Now you've got audience members who have probably worked all day and are getting tired. They may also have been visiting the cash bar before dinner, and wine may be served during dinner. So now you've got an audience that may be so relaxed they're nodding off in the poppy seed salad dressing. Like the late evening keynote speaker, you're going to need a large infusion of entertainer style to keep them awake and with you. (You may also have to deal with cranky drunks.)

Presentation Style

As we said before, your choice of style will depend primarily on the time of day for your after-food presentation. Breakfast and lunch programs can be a bit more on the professorial side—more lecture, more learning. Dinner programs, on the other hand, will require more humor, more jazzy visuals, and far less lecturing. They'll need mostly Entertainer, with a significant measure of Orator and Preacher, and a little bit of Facilitator.

Take your cue from Mark Twain. The noted author of such American classics as *Tom Sawyer* and *Huckleberry Finn*, Twain was frequently invited to speak at such after-dinner events as the 1882 77th Annual Dinner of the New England Society of New York, celebrating the anniversary of the pilgrims' landing at Plymouth Rock.

The dinner was attended by 250 members of the society and their friends, all men. The eating ended at (can you believe this?) 9 p.m., and then the attendees all lit up cigars (cough, cough) and (we assume) beamed contentedly through a whole series of "toasts," of which Twain's was the last. His "toast" was actually a 45-minute long satire comparing the fashion habits of "the savage woman of Central Africa" and "the daughter of modern civilization." As reported in the next day's *New York Times*, Twain's speech was a big hit, despite the fact that it must have been nearly 11:00 p.m. by the time he finished. Just imagine what kind of reviews he would have gotten if he had pulled out a stack of densely-designed overhead transparencies, turned to the screen, pulled out his pointer, and droned on about data and dates for three-quarters of an hour! [Note: For more about Twain's speaking appearances, see Chapter 10.]

> *5 Quick Tips for After-Dinner Talks with Style:*
> 1. Consider the constraints of the time of day. Don't go on too long late at night and definitely avoid lecturing in the evening.
> 2. Write your own introduction to avoid any unpleasant surprises.
> 3. Ignore the wait staff as they bus the tables. No one will remember that they were there. 4. Add humor for an after-dinner talk; add more instruction for a breakfast or lunch program.
> 4. Learn as much as you can about the group you will be presenting to and then work references to their organization into your presentation.

Public Hearings with Style

Who

Who typically shows up at a public hearing? Really committed people. People with a cause. People with an axe to grind. People with a complaint. No one attends a public hearing because they have to (except the speakers). You can therefore expect an extremely interested, highly motivated audience.

Unfortunately, they may be highly motivated by their own opinions and not at all interested in actually hearing what you have to say. "It's a public HEARING," they'll say. "You're supposed to be here to LISTEN TO US. We don't need to listen to YOU." They may even speak in a language you don't understand. We once observed a public hearing where most of the audience members spoke Navajo. At a particularly tense moment in the proceedings, an audience member took the microphone, spoke at length in Navajo, and the rest of the audience howled with laughter. The speaker didn't have a clue as to what was so funny, but you can bet the joke was on him.

They may be right. The name "public hearing" does indeed suggest that the purpose of the event is to hear what the public has to say, not to make the public hear what you have to say. So you need to be prepared to deal with strongly-opinionated, outspoken individuals. You're not going to make these people happy; you're not going to make them love you; so don't even try. (You'll be lucky if they just wind up respecting you, instead of riding you out of town on a rail.)

What

If the objective of the public hearing is truly to hear the public, then you'd better keep your own remarks to a minimum and allow as much time as you can for the Q&A. The Presentation Diamond™ will thus look like this:

Notice how concise all the sections are. Your opening and close should be extremely short. Just say hello, introduce yourself quickly, then get right to the objective and focus of the hearing. After the Q&A (and be prepared for them to go over time), do your best to paraphrase what you have heard, tell them what's going to happen next, say thank you and goodbye. Then be prepared to hang around for as long as individual participants want to talk to you.

[Note: Certain organizations, like the Securities and Exchange Commission, or other governmental agencies, have very strict rules governing the structure of their public hearings. Information about these rules can be found on the Internet.]

Where

Public hearings are usually held in public places. (Makes sense, doesn't it?) Venues can include town hall meeting rooms, auditoriums, and the like. Typically, the room setup is not conducive to a relaxed interchange of expressions; on the contrary, you're more apt to find yourself on a real stage, far above and away from where the audience is sitting in "theater seats" fastened to the floor.

If you find yourself relegated to this circumstance, don't despair. There is still one important change you can make to the space to increase the chance of establishing rapport with your audience: GET DOWN OFF THE STAGE. Set your stuff up (long table, perhaps, if there are several presenters) in front of the stage, on the same level as the members of the audience. This removes the sense that you are "above" them in your "castle," separated from them by a "moat" of differences. (Once you stand up, they'll all be able to see you.) Do not let the logistics undermine your attempts at establishing camaraderie with your audience.

When

Public hearings could be scheduled at any time of the day, including after normal business hours, so that audience members can attend after work. The time of day won't matter much to the audience for a public hearing; when they're upset about something, they tend not to doze off.

You do need to be realistic about how much actual time you've allotted for the hearing itself. Don't imagine that you can get by with a 10 minute presentation (including the Q&A) if the focus of the hearing is on "Plans to Build a Mega Giant Super Store in the Middle of Your Quiet Rural Community." You'll need at least an hour, most of it devoted to collecting comments and complaints.

Presentation Style

Avoid the Entertainer style, unless it feels completely right to inject a teensy bit of humor to help defuse tension. (And you'd better be sure it will work, or you will certainly make the situation worse.) Very rarely should you choose Orator, either. (Remember that they've come to be heard, not to hear.) And Professor could backfire on you if you come across as a pompous lecturer who purports to know more than they do.

No, definitely a little Preacher to start things off and then a lot of Facilitator are the styles that will be most effective in a public hearing. You want to convince them of the sincerity of your concern (the Preacher part), but mostly you want them to vent their feelings in a productive way (the Facilitator part). If you can figure out a way to get them into groups and then debrief, all well and good. This will prevent one or two particularly outspoken individuals from hogging the spotlight.

---

5 Quick Tips for Public Hearing with Style:

1. You're not there to make them love you, so don't even try. Just assure them of your concern and maintain your professionalism.
2. Do not lecture; facilitate instead.
3. Be prepared for audience members to want to go over the scheduled time limit. Try to accommodate them.
4. Remove all "barriers" (actual and spatial) between you and your audience.
5. Paraphrase their comments to their satisfaction. Then follow through on whatever action you've promised them.

Instructional Sessions with Style

Who

Audiences members will be people who (mostly) will want to learn something. This is true for the most part for adults, but not always. Sometimes your participants may have been "sent" by a supervisor who has noticed a deficiency in their work performance. Sometimes you might have people who are just glad to get some time off work, and view the session as a holiday. (Professional trainers call these kind of people "tourists.")

In any case, serious students and tourists alike will be gratified if you accomplish two things:

1. You actually teach them something.
2. You keep them awake and interested while they're learning.

The problems occur when, as usually happens, you have that good old "mixed" audience of students: some who know nothing, some who know a little, and some who think they know everything. You can advertise certain prerequisites for your session, but that won't guarantee that the wrong students may show up.

What

The objective for an instructional session is typically procedural: "How to Deal with a Toxic Spill"; "How to Drive Defensively"; "How to Punctuate Correctly"; "How to Manage Information Effectively"; etc. Instructional designers typically prefer to state the objective using the SWBA pattern: "After this class, Students Will Be Able to…." This pattern requires you to focus on the outcome of the instruction, rather than on the quality of the presentation. Remember, if you merely keep your students awake and interested, but you don't actually teach them anything, you will have wasted everyone's time.

Here is the Presentation Diamond™ for an instructional session:

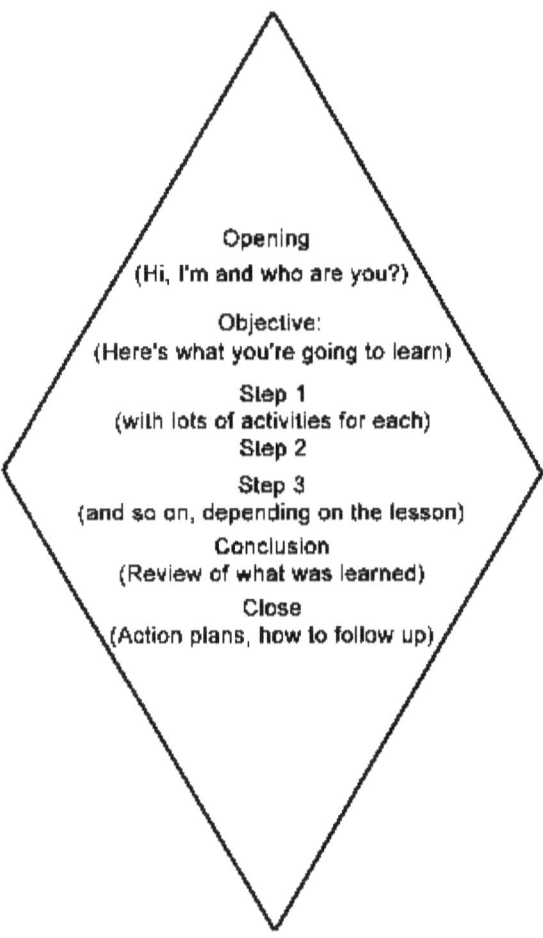

Opening
(Hi, I'm and who are you?)

Objective:
(Here's what you're going to learn)

Step 1
(with lots of activities for each)
Step 2

Step 3
(and so on, depending on the lesson)
Conclusion
(Review of what was learned)
Close
(Action plans, how to follow up)

Instructional sessions can be lengthy (5 days at a time) or short (10 minutes), depending on the process being taught. If you've got lots of time, you can include all kinds of interactive activities to build rapport and enhance learning. You can, for example, structure your opening so that it is actually an exercise in which you get the audience to talk to each other and share concerns. (These kinds of activities are usually called "icebreakers." See Chapter 10.) You can do the same with your close. You can also devise a conclusion in which the students review what they have learned by playing some sort of a game, like Jeopardy, which tests their knowledge acquisition. And then, of course, you can add all kinds of activities (such as simulations and problem-solving scenarios) to help them learn the actual steps of the process. About the only part of the session that will remain relatively brief is the objective.

You'll note also that we have not included a formal Q&A session here. The reason should be obvious: In an instructional session, you want to encourage your participants to ask questions throughout the presentation, especially as they think of them. Plus, seasoned trainers know that it's pretty much never a good idea to ask for questions at the end of a training session. Everyone wants to leave, and they're going to throw dirty looks toward any participant who might be so stupid as to actually ask a question at closing time.

Where

Anywhere. You can teach people in a classroom, an auditorium, a meeting room, out in the parking lot, or up a tree—it just depends on what it is you're teaching. (If your topic is "How to Drive a Tank through Enemy Lines," we're guessing that you're not going to be spending too much time in a classroom!)

[The Future is Now Note: We do realize, however, that simulations are becoming more common, and soon you'll actually be able to learn how to drive a tank through enemy lines without leaving the safety of your classroom and computer program.]

The main thing to consider when conducting an instructional session is how the materials you've prepared will be used in the actual training. For example, if you're planning on giving them exercises to fill out with paper and pen, then you'd better make sure they have something to write on. If you expect them to do a lot of small-group discussion and problem-solving, then you should arrange the room in clusters. Ask yourself, "Under what conditions will my students be participating in the learning experience?" and then make sure you set up the space and design the materials to accommodate those conditions.

When

Any time of the day, even in the middle of the night, if you're conducting an on-the-job session for people who work swing shift. And so here's another good reason why you should include as many hands-on exercises as possible: You never know what condition your trainees may be in, whether they've gotten any rest, so you need to do everything you can to keep them awake and alert.

Presentation Style

A large amount of Professor, to be sure, is important for an instructional session. After all, they have come to you to learn from you. But too much Professor over a long period of time can be deadly. So add a significant amount of Facilitator: Ask them questions, encourage them to comment, and get them into activities whenever appropriate. And sprinkle generous helpings of Entertainer throughout a particularly lengthy session to keep them awake and having fun. A little bit of Preacher and a little bit of Orator could be nice, too, especially at the right moments when you really want them to remember what you said.

Think about it: The best teachers you had in school were probably adept mixtures of all 5 styles. No one needs to be more flexible than a teacher!

---

5 Quick Tips for Instructional Sessions with Style:

1. Design your session to take advantage of the space.
2. Reach all your students by using a mix of audio-visual aids, and both verbal and visual illustrations.
3. Include exercises and activities to involve them and enhance their retention.
4. Add humor and drama to keep them awake and learning.
5. Devise strategies for follow up after the instruction.

Note: The best book we know on how to make an instructional session exciting and memorable is Ellen's *The Standup Trainer*. (See Chapter 10 for details.)

Continuously Improve Your Style

Becoming a superior presenter is like becoming a superior violinist: You never reach complete perfection, but you keep trying to come close.

There are three main ways to continually polish your presentation skills:

1. Read books about presenting.
2. Watch others present.
3. Present yourself.

All three have their benefits. Let's examine them.

1. Read books.

Well, obviously we think this is a good idea, since we've written a book and we feel pretty sure that you're reading it at this moment. But seriously, you can learn lots of useful tips and tricks from books on presentation skills, some of which we've included in Chapter 10.

You can also find useful information about presentation skills on the Internet, and we've listed some sites we like in Chapter 10 as well.

Just remember that other books on presentation skills do not distinguish the varying needs of the different presentation styles as we've described them in this book. Books that focus on adding humor to a presentation, for example, frequently suggest material that would hardly be suitable for any audience or situation, let alone for your presentation style. You need to pick and choose material and approaches that suit your own comfort level.

2. Watch others present.

This is an excellent way to hone your skills. You can watch another presenter and say to yourself, "That's fabulous, what he or she just did. I've got to remember to do that in my next presentation." Or, "That's terrible! I've got to remember NEVER to do that in front of an audience." Both good and bad examples are learning examples.

So where do you find presenters to watch? Some are on TV (although most of these are not just exhibiting Preacher styles—they're actual preachers!); some are on video. Best, though, is to watch a live performance, and you can find these most easily at professional society conferences. Go ahead, be one of those audience members who sits in the back of the room and leaves early. Then you can arrive late at another presentation, leave early from that, and so on. Not the most courteous behavior in the world, we agree, but this will give you the greatest exposure to a number of different presentation styles.

As you watch someone make a live presentation (or a dead one, we don't care), try to assess what presentation style is being primarily manifested. Then decide if that particular style is indeed the best choice, given the specific audience and the particular situation (including time of day). This exercise will help you enhance your own presentation flexibility.

If you can stand it, try analyzing the presentation styles of various politicians. What about Al Gore's style, for example? People have complained that he is too "wooden" as a speaker. Too much a Professor? Should he add more Entertainer? Or Preacher? And what does this analysis suggest about politics in general—that people respond better, say, to Entertainers than Professors? That they vote more often for Orators? (For a further discussion of this point, see Chapter 10.)

3. Present yourself.

There's no escaping it: Practice does make for closer to perfect. The more you present, the more you learn about your own abilities as a presenter. Thus, it's also important to seek out opportunities to present in a wide variety of circumstances. If you exclusively present at company staff meetings, for example, all you'll get is pretty good at presenting at company staff meetings. You'll lack the versatility evidenced by the best presenters.

So beside those staff meetings, where can you present? At professional conferences, of course. Join a society or two, and submit a proposal to speak at a conference or simply volunteer to speak at a monthly program. This will be very good experience, as you'll be speaking to your own peers, always a tough (but extremely useful for learning) audience.

Then, for variety, seek out other speaking opportunities, like at your church, or the local community center, or a local school. (You want to speak in front of the world's most difficult audience? Then volunteer to make a presentation to a class of junior high school students.)

And then, if you really feel brave, and if you are determined to up your entertainer ante, go to a local comedy club on "open mike night" and try your hand at a bit of real standup comedy. We guarantee that you will find the experience incredibly educational.

No matter how or when you present, you'll need to constantly evaluate yourself if you want to constantly improve. Use the following assessment tool to do just that:

Evaluating for Continuous Improvement

Presentation aspect	*What worked?*	*What didn't work?*	*What should I do differently next time?*
My Presentation Style			
My Presentation Material			
My Presentation Design and Timing			
My Preparation			
My "Performance Skills"			
My Rapport with my Audience			
My Ability to Deal with the Unexpected			
My Skill at Presenting a Specific Kind of Presentation			

7 Not-So-Quick Tips for Polishing Your Presentation Style:

1. Take voice lessons.
2. Join a choir.
3. Audition for a part in a community theater production.
4. Volunteer to be a storyteller for kids at your local library or public school.
5. Exercise your body so that you feel comfortable moving it around in space.
6. Take a dance class.
7. Sign up for Jazzercise™ (exercise and dance class combined).

Notice that none of these are "quick" fixes. But all will prove productive over time, guaranteed.

"The best laid plans of mice and men," as the poet Robbie Burns once said, "oft go astray." Without an action plan, you'll most likely agree that these ideas for improvement are all good and useful, and then you'll forget about them. So to keep your eyes on the prize, try filling out the following Action Plan for continual improvement.

Action Plan for Presenters with Style

I [your name here], being of not necessarily sound, but close to it, mind and also somewhat sound, depending on how much exercise I've gotten lately, body, do solemnly (with only a little giggling) swear to do the following to improve my presentation skills:

1. I promise to build a presentation style that will work best for me under a variety of circumstances. I also promise to try a bit of my least preferred style whenever possible and appropriate. (For example, if I am an Entertainer by preference, I promise to add a bit of, say, Facilitator whenever I can.)

2. I promise to find material that will liven up my presentations and yet be true to my presentation style. I promise to tell stories more frequently (when appropriate). I promise to create Power Point presentations that will NOT put my audience into a trance.

3. I promise to design presentations that are logically structured and accurately timed. I promise NEVER to go over my time limit, unless forced to by my entire audience.

4. I promise to always arrive at my presentation site early so that I can effectively "set the stage" for my audience. I also promise to spend all my pre-performance time worrying about their needs, rather than my own butterflies.

5. I promise to investigate ways to move appropriately in front of an audience. I promise to speak loudly enough for everyone to hear me and with enough vocal variety to keep everyone awake.

6. I promise to make every attempt to establish immediate rapport with my audience. I promise to investigate ways to make every presentation I make participatory, no matter how big the room or how large the audience.

7. I promise to stay in character no matter what happens during my presentation. I also promise to deal with any "bad" audience members in an effective and courteous way.

8. I promise to apply the lessons I have learned from this book to a variety of presentation situations, always remembering that flexibility is the key to success.

9. I promise to read more, watch more, and present more.

10. I promise to stop making so many promises and just get out there AND DO IT!

Signed this _____ day of _____, in the year _____,

_____

Research & Resources

This chapter is not a bibliography (although it contains some bibliographic references). It's not a *Chicken Soup for the Presenter's Soul* (although it includes some inspirational stories). It's not a compendium of jokes (although it contains some funny stuff). It's not an appendix (although it includes some supplemental information). It's sort of all of these combined. We like to think of this section as a collection of things we mentioned in passing in the book that maybe you would like to know a little more about.

Welcome to our *Research & Resources Hodgepodge.*

* **Want to get a hold of the best book, bar none, on the art of injecting humor and drama into any dry instructional session?** Then race your fingers right over to amazon.com to purchase *The Standup Trainer* by Ellen Dowling (1995). Like stage actors and standup comics, technical presenters and trainers perform before a live audience. This book shares theatrical secrets that can enliven learning and enhance presentation skills: how to move and gesture dramatically, how to deal with difficult audience members, and how to create and develop humorous material. A guaranteed cure for boring technical presentations!

* **Who was Constantin Stanislavsky?** He was a Russian theatrical director, teacher, and actor, whose original name was Constantin Sergeyevich Alekseyev, and he lived from 1863-1938. He was cofounder with Vladimir Nemirovich-Danchenko of the Moscow Art Theater in 1898, which he would remain associated with for remainder of life. He also achieved renown as a director of opera. As a director, he stressed ensemble acting as well as complete coordination of all phases of production. His outstanding productions included many of the plays of Chekhov, in which he tried to strip away rhetorical clichés to enter the emotional core and complex psychology of the characters. Stanislavsky stressed the importance of the actor's inner identification with the character and the actor's natural use of body and voice. His training, now termed the Stanislavsky method, or "method" acting, had a vast influence on modern schools of acting. In New York City the Actors' Studio adapted many of his ideas to their use. See Stanislavsky's *An Actor Prepares* (tr. 1936), *Building a Character* (tr. 1950), and *Creating a Role* (tr. 1961); his autobiographical *My Life in Art* (tr. 1924); biography by Elena Polyakova (1982); studies by Christine Edwards, *The Stanislavsky Heritage* (1965); Sonia Moore, *The Stanislavksy System* (1974); and Nikolai Gorchakov, *Stanislavsky Directs* (1968, repr. 1974). [Note: All of these books—and more!—are available from amazon.com.]

The Columbia Encyclopedia, Fifth Edition Copyright ©1993, Columbia University Press.

* **Want to add elegance and clarity to your visual aids (especially your PowerPoint presentations)?** Then you must investigate Edward R. Tufte's *The Quantitative Display of Visual Information*, reprinted 1992. From amazon.com's editorial review: "A timeless classic in how complex information should be presented graphically. The *Strunk & White* of visual design. Should occupy a place of honor—within arm's reach—of everyone attempting to understand or depict numerical data graphically. The design of the book is an exemplar of the principles it espouses: elegant typography and layout, and seamless integration of lucid text and perfectly chosen graphical examples. Very Highly Recommended."

* **Looking for stories and anecdotes to spice up your presentation?** Check out Joe Griffith, editor, *Speaker's Library of Business Stories, Anecdotes, and Humor.* (Prentice-Hall, 1990.) Amazon.com's synopsis: "From Vince Lombardi's inspiring talk on commitment to hilarious

one-liners about honesty, here's a collection of both fresh and classic stories, quotes, analogies and examples that will add punch and vividness to any business speaker's repertoire."

Another source for amazing-but-true stories is Randy Cassingham's e-mail newsletter, *This is True*, available by subscription (there's a free version available) by sending a blank message to join@thisistrue.com or visiting their web site at www.thisistrue.com. They have also begun a companion site, called *Heroic Stories* (www.HeroicStories.com), which contains stories that many Orators and Preachers will find useful.

We get a kick out of true stories about real idiots. If you're like us (we hope you are), then you'll definitely need to become a subscriber to Scott Adams' *Dilbert Newsletter*. You can sign up for the free *Dilbert Newsletter* automatically. Send a blank e-mail to dilbert-text-on@list.unitedmedia.com. Then you, too, can gather Dogbert's "True Tales of In-Duh-viduals" to use in your presentations.

And don't forget to use the Web as a primary resource for collecting stories and anecdotes. For example, last year we found a collection of travel horror stories (entitled "Travelers Find Giggles in Their Travails") on *USA Today's* web site (www.usatoday.com). Here is a sample:

> From Jeanette Eatherly, New Orleans:
> I was running through Chicago's O'Hare to make a flight when I came upon a smiling, young male security attendant. I hurriedly explained that I have a pacemaker, expecting to be waved around the rope barrier and patted down by a female attendant. (I'd been advised that passing through the X-ray detector could affect the pacemaker's settings.) Instead, he looked at me and asked, "Do you have it with you?"

* **Want some inspirational stories for your next speech?** Here are a few:

Those Amazing Amoebas

Researchers in California placed amoebas in two tanks. In one tank, the temperature, humidity, level of water, and other conditions were constantly adjusted to provide the environment most conducive for proliferation of the amoeba. In another tank, the organisms were alternately subjected to extremes in heat and cold, fluid level, protein, etc.

To the researcher's amazement, the amoebas in the tank meant to induce rapid growth died faster than those subjected to extremes. The researchers theorized that having things too perfect, too set, too comfortable actually causes us to decay and die, while being forced to adapt promotes growth.

The Point of this Story: What doesn't kill us, makes us stronger.

A Close Shave

Legend has it that Albert Einstein kept a small sign taped to the bottom of his bathroom mirror. The sign said, "Shave slowly."

Einstein frequently worked on problems while he was sleeping. He'd "tell" his brain to work on the problem, go to sleep, get up the next morning, go to the bathroom, and begin shaving with his straight razor. (These are the days before Bic.) Invariably, the solution to his problem would come to him while he was shaving, hence the need for the sign, "Shave slowly." Without it, Einstein might have slit his own throat!

The Point of this Story: You can "direct" your unconscious mind to solve problems; just don't kill yourself when you come up with the answer.

The Story of the Stressed-Out Rats

Professor N. R. F. Maier of the University of Michigan performed a series of interesting experiments to induce neuroses in rats. In the study, the rats were trained to jump at one of two doors. If they jumped to the right, they would bump their noses and fall into the net. If they jumped to the left, the door would open and they would get food. The rats learned pretty quickly to always jump to the left.

Then one day the experimenters (we could call them "upper management") decided to change the rules of the game. (This never happens in your company, does it?) That day, when the rats reported for maze work, they suddenly found that they had to jump now at the *right* door to get food, instead of the left. The rats were a bit upset at first, but they soon got used to the change and learned to always jump to the right. (Is this beginning to sound familiar?)

Then the fiendish bosses decided to make the rules even more capricious and arbitrary. Some days when the rats came to work they had to jump to the right to get food; other days they had to jump to the left. The rats would never know, on any given day, which was the food door. As you can imagine, this caused the rats major distress. In fact, they got so stressed out that soon they refused to jump at all. They just sat there.

So the bosses decided to force the rats to make a choice. They hit them with blasts of air and electric shocks.

This torture so freaked the rats out that they all fell into what is called a "fixated" state, where one repeats the same action over and over, never mind the consequences. In this state, a rat will continuously jump at the left door and bump his nose, even though *the right door is open and the food is clearly visible!*

When the bosses persisted in forcing the rats to make what appeared to them to be hopeless choices, they eventually went into convulsions, raced around wildly, bumped into things, and finally fell into a coma. In this state, the rats refused to eat, refused to take an interest in anything. They could be rolled up into balls or suspended in the air by their legs. These rats ceased to care what happened to them. They had a "nervous breakdown."

The Point of This Story: Do you feel in control of your own environment? Who's pulling your strings? (And what can you do about it?)

Want more? Visit the Professional Training Company's web site at http://www.protrainco.com/info/essays/tellstory.htm

* **How to find quotations to use in your presentations:**
    1. Investigate quotation collections, especially the most famous, *Bartlett's Familiar Quotations*, originally compiled by John Bartlett in 1901, and now in its 9th edition. For the online search engine, just go to http://www.bartleby.com/99/

2. Start a collection of your own. Jot down things you hear others say, or things you read in various compilations. (If you are a George Carlin, fan, for example, you'll want to peruse his latest book, *Brain Droppings*, for some pretty cool quotes. One of our personal favorites is the humorist Fran Leibowitz, author of *The Fran Leibowitz Reader*. This paperback collects her two bestsellers of the 1970s her two bestsellers of the 1970s, *Metropolitan Life and Social Studies*, into one volume The pieces still hold up as good writing and deliver plenty of sharp laughs.)

* **Is your voice too high, too nasal, too grating? Do you speak too softly or too loud? Want to learn how to enunciate more precisely and project more effectively?** Then check out the actor's bible of vocal dexterity, Cicely Berry's *Voice and the Actor*, reprinted 1991. Amazon.com says: "*Voice and the Actor* covers everything actors need to know about controlling the voice, their most important instrument. It includes detailed, clear exercises and explanations on developing a natural stage voice, breathing, enunciation, and pitch and timbre, with special advice on difficult delivery problems."

* **Are you interested in learning more about proxemics, the study of how spatial relationships affect communication?** Then you must begin with Edward T. Hall's *The Hidden Dimension* (reprinted 1992). Publisher's description: "An examination of various cultural concepts of space and how differences among them affect modern society. Introducing the science of *proxemics*, Hall demonstrates how man's use of space can affect personal business relations, cross-cultural exchanges, architecture, city planning, and urban renewal." This is THE book to help you understand how a presenter with style can manipulate the space to communicate most effectively with an audience.

* Although we find most **books on presentation skills** to be repetitious, sometimes irrelevant, and frequently not very useful (our book, of course, is the notable exception!), we do recommend Ron Hoff's *I Can*

See You Naked, revised 1992. We like it for the same reason described by an amazon.com reader from Cleveland, Ohio: "I used to be a nervous wreck. Making my oral presentation for my undergraduate honors thesis almost did me in. My sister gave me this book to be funny, but I read it to learn. I found this book helpful, not only for letting me see group presentations in a different light, but also for the insights it gave me for other social situations." So this is the book you want if you're just starting out and suffering from severe stage fright. (You'll remember, from our preface, that *Presenting with Style* is for experienced presenters who don't find stage fright to be a big deal anymore.)

    * **Looking for some good one-liners to use in sticky situations?** Take a peek at Lilly Walters' *What to Say When . . .You're Dying on the Platform* (1995). A testimonial from a satisfied amazon.com reviewer: "I picked up this title on a whim one day and it has turned out to be one of the most valuable resources I have. Did you ever wonder how to handle those speaking disasters that always seem to come at THE worst time?...like your mic failing, or someone becoming ill, or your plane is late, or you have a terrible cold? Walters has collected some excellent advice on what to say, what to do, and most importantly, what *NOT* to say or do when these things happen."

    * **Want to know more about the concept of Open Space Technology for conferences?** Open Space Technology is the most powerful leadership approach for the 21st Century. Developed by organizational consultant Harrison Owen from Potomac, Maryland, USA, it taps into the spirit of an organization like no other large or small group intervention can. It is now used around the world to enable organizations to learn and achieve beyond their expectations with a simple approach, based on clear values and principles. Open Space creates an environment for innovation, problem solving, creativity, team work, and rapid change. For more information, visit http://www.openspacetechnology.com/about.html.

    * **Want to know more about Mark Twain's talent as an after-dinner speaker?** According to the chronology at the end of Paul Fatout's

Mark Twain Speaking, in the course of his career MT gave over 150 after-dinner speeches. The typical context for one of these performances was a lavish dinner, in honor of someone (like Whittier) or something (like the landing on Plymouth Rock), attended mainly by male notables. A couple hours of eating and drinking was followed by a couple of hours of ceremonial toasting, which allowed for more drinking and also fed the era's appetite for oratory. As comic relief to the standard grandiloquent rhetoric, MT was invited to many of these dinners. By the end of his career "Mark Twain" was himself the guest of honor at such affairs. Although they were exhausting events, he never lost his enthusiasm for being there and, when his turn came, "making the tables roar with laughter," as newspaper reports often put it. By starting with the 1882 toast "To Woman," you can get an idea how much of his care and energy MT invested in these ephemeral performances. The full toast is reproduced on this web site: http://etext.virginia.edu/railton/onstage/speeches.html.

* **Want to know about some organizations/professional societies that can give you opportunities to practice your presentation style?**

The American Society for Training and Development (ASTD) provides annual conferences and local chapters where professionals can practicing speaking to their peers on a variety of educational subjects (www.astd.org). The International Society for Performance Improvement (ISPI) does likewise (www.ispi.org).

The National Speakers Association (www.nsaspeaker.org) is the preeminent forum for those who profess to be professional speakers. To become a member, you must be willing to prove that you are not just speaking as a hobby—you must provide evidence that you have earned a substantial amount of money as a speaker during the previous year.

If you're just starting out, and if stage fright is your bane, then you definitely need to find the nearest Toastmasters group (www.toastmasters.org). At Toastmasters, members learn by speaking to groups and working with others in a supportive environment. A typical

Toastmasters club is made up of 20 to 30 people who meet once a week for about an hour. Each meeting gives everyone an opportunity to practice a variety of speaking situations.

* **Want to know how to increase your Facilitator skills and make your presentations more participatory? Need some ideas for interactive exercises (such as icebreakers)?** Surely the "Father of Participatory Training" is Bob Pike, owner of Creative Training Techniques, Inc. (http://www.creativetrainingtech.com/). Through his company, you can sign up for workshops and conferences that will provide you with loads of tools for increasing audience involvement. You can also purchase products on his site, including **The Standup Trainer** (which is co-published by CTT).

There are also a score of books available that list hundreds of interactive games and activities that you might be able to adapt to your particular style and situation. Among the best of these are

> *Warmups for Meeting Leaders* by Sue Bianchi, Jan Butler, David Richey (Pfeiffer, 1990).
>
> *The Big Book of Business Games : Icebreakers, Creativity Exercises and Meeting Energizers (Games Trainers Play Series)* by Edward Scannell (Contributor), John W. Newstrom (McGraw-Hill, 1966).
>
> *100 Training Games* by Gary Kroehnert (McGraw-Hill, 1992).
>
> *Great Session Openers, Closers, and Energizers: Quick Activities for Warming Up Your Audience and Ending on a High Note* by Marlene Caroselli (McGraw-Hill, 1998).

Of course, you can always just e-mail Ellen Dowling (edowling@standuptrainer.com) and she'll be happy to help you devise an activity that would be just perfect for you (and for your audience).

* **And for some further reading:**

Enlivening IDL Instruction, by Jodi Reed. (American Society for Training and Development *Technical Training Journal*, May/June 1999, pp. 28-30.) "Interactive Distance Learning is not the passive experience of its familiar-looking cousin, television," says the author. "But many

learners have a difficult time changing ingrained habits and precon-
ceptions produced by years of television-viewing experience." The
solution? Add a little Entertainer and a lot of Facilitator! Or, in Jodi
Reed's words, "Engage students with variety and interaction."

"Incorporate variety into instruction to keep interest and motivation
high. Even with thrilling visuals and instructors, nobody wants to watch
a talking head for hours, so make sure learners have an opportunity to
focus attention away from the screen…. Highly motivated learners in a
tightly focused lesson can tolerate lengthy lectures, but as a rule of
thumb, don't lecture for more than 15 minutes at one time. Instead,
alternate lectures with activities or discussions."

Breathing Life into Dull Safety Training Sessions, by Susan Boyd.
(American Society for Training and Development *Technical Training
Journal*, March/April 1999, p. 37.) "Safety training presents some
unique challenges," according to the author. "While the topics may be
critical and even save lives, the learners often view the training as dry,
boring, and unrelated to their needs." The solution? Start with an
Entertainer/Facilitator! "Start off with a short opening exercise or dramatic example that gets the learners involved right away." Want an
example of a "dramatic example"? "For personal protective equipment
(PPE), put an apple under a hard hat and hit it with a heavy object, then
remove the hard hat and hit it again to show the importance of the right
protection." (A little Gallagher, anyone?)

And since we're writing this in the year 2000, an election year, we
can't resist mentioning a couple of recent articles that discuss the presentation styles of two of the presidential candidates:

Bush's Verbal Stumblings Cause for Amusement, Bemusement by
Ron Hutcheson, Knight Rider Newspapers, printed in *The
Albuquerque Journal*, January 29, 2000. In this article, the author
reports on a number of recent cases where George W. Bush,
Republican presidential candidate, has mangled his meaning. "At a
breakfast meeting with the Nashua Chamber of Commerce, Bush

illustrated his brand of compassionate conservativism by urging his listeners to put themselves in the role of a single mother 'working hard to put food on your family.'" Later, at a nearby elementary school, whose students were promoting *perseverance* as the character trait of the month, Bush declared, "This is preservation month. I appreciate preservation. It's what you do when you run for president—you gotta preserve." And later, at another venue, instead of knocking down tariffs and trade barriers, Bush said he intends to eliminate "terriers."

"Does any of this matter, politically speaking?" asks Hutcheson. "Pundits say it might, if only because voters expect a more polished performance." Of course they do—they expect a polished Orator.

Where's the Music? by Joe Klein. (*The New Yorker*, September 27, 1999, pp. 36-42.) The premise of this article is Klein's question, "If, as we are ceaselessly told, there has been a collision of politics, celebrity, and entertainment, why are the people who are running for President in the emptily portentous year 2000 so crashingly dull?" Where is "the inspiration of Franklin Roosevelt, the spontaneity of Harry Truman, the eloquence of Adlai Stevenson, the dash of John Kennedy"? What's missing? "It is style, far more than substance, that is missing from our bleached, anorexic contemporary politics. It is playfulness and eloquence, charm and musicality, spontaneity and passion and inspiration." In other words, we've got a whole bunch of Professors running for office, when what we really want is an Entertainer/Preacher/Orator.

About the Authors

Ellen Dowling, PhD, has been knocking 'em dead in the classroom, in the training room, in the auditorium, in the club, and on the stage for over 30 years. She has been a high school teacher, a college professor, a folksinger, an actor, a playwright, a director, and a standup comic.

Currently, she is President of **Dowling & Associates, Inc.** based in Albuquerque, New Mexico. She is a nationally known speaker and consultant who conducts training programs in writing, public speaking, and interpersonal skills for a variety of clients, including Intel Corporation; Maybelline, Inc.; Honeywell; Security First Technologies; General Mills; and Alltel. A member of the American Society for Training and Development (ASTD) since 1983, Dr. Dowling has held many leadership positions at both local and regional levels.

She is also the author of *The Standup Trainer*, published in 1995 by ASTD and Bob Pike's Creative Training Techniques, Inc., and available for ordering from amazon.com.

To contact Ellen Dowling, e-mail her at edowling@standuptrainer.com.

Michael Dowling, PhD, is Professor of Innovation and Technology Management at the University of Regensburg, Germany. Formerly he was an Associate Professor in the School of Business at the University of Georgia where he taught presentation techniques to MBA and undergraduate students. He has published articles in *Strategic Management Journal, Management Science, California Management Review, Business Horizons, and Columbia Journal of World Business.*

In great demand as an international conference presenter and executive education instructor, Dr. Dowling has also consulted with various companies and organizations including Bell South Corporation, Southwestern Bell, UBM Consulting, and the National Broadcasting Company.

To contact Michael Dowling, e-mail him at michael.dowling@wiwi.uni-regensburg.de or visit his web page at www.wiwi.uni-regensburg.de/dowling/

[Note: In case you haven't figured this out by now, Dr. Ellen Dowling and Dr. Mike Dowling are sister and brother.]